On
Reinventing HR

HBR's 10 Must Reads series is the definitive collection of ideas and best practices for aspiring and experienced leaders alike. These books offer essential reading selected from the pages of *Harvard Business Review* on topics critical to the success of every manager.

Titles include:

HBR's 10 Must Reads 2015
HBR's 10 Must Reads 2016
HBR's 10 Must Reads 2017
HBR's 10 Must Reads 2018
HBR's 10 Must Reads 2019
HBR's 10 Must Reads 2020
HBR's 10 Must Reads for CEOs
HBR's 10 Must Reads for New Managers
HBR's 10 Must Reads on AI, Analytics, and the New Machine Age
HBR's 10 Must Reads on Business Model Innovation
HBR's 10 Must Reads on Change Management
HBR's 10 Must Reads on Collaboration
HBR's 10 Must Reads on Communication
HBR's 10 Must Reads on Diversity
HBR's 10 Must Reads on Emotional Intelligence
HBR's 10 Must Reads on Entrepreneurship and Startups
HBR's 10 Must Reads on Innovation
HBR's 10 Must Reads on Leadership
HBR's 10 Must Reads on Leadership for Healthcare
HBR's 10 Must Reads on Leadership Lessons from Sports
HBR's 10 Must Reads on Making Smart Decisions
HBR's 10 Must Reads on Managing Across Cultures
HBR's 10 Must Reads on Managing People
HBR's 10 Must Reads on Managing Yourself
HBR's 10 Must Reads on Mental Toughness
HBR's 10 Must Reads on Negotiation
HBR's 10 Must Reads on Nonprofits and the Social Sectors

On
Reinventing
HR

HARVARD BUSINESS REVIEW PRESS
Boston, Massachusetts

Copyright 2019 Harvard Business School Publishing Corporation
All rights reserved
Printed in the United States of America
10 9 8 7 6 5 4 3 2 1

The web addresses referenced in this book were live and correct at the time of the book's publication but may be subject to change.

Cataloging-in-Publication data is forthcoming.

ISBN: 978-1-63369-784-3   **33614081428509**
eISBN: 978-1-63369-785-0

Contents

On
Reinventing HR

People Before Strategy

A New Role for the CHRO. **by Ram Charan, Dominic Barton, and Dennis Carey**

CEOs KNOW THAT they depend on their company's human resources to achieve success. Businesses don't create value; people do. But if you peel back the layers at the vast majority of companies, you find CEOs who are distanced from and often dissatisfied with their chief human resources officers (CHROs) and the HR function in general. Research by McKinsey and the Conference Board consistently finds that CEOs worldwide see human capital as a top challenge, and they rank HR as only the eighth or ninth most important function in a company. That has to change.

It's time for HR to make the same leap that the finance function has made in recent decades and become a true partner to the CEO. Just as the CFO helps the CEO lead the business by raising and allocating financial resources, the CHRO should help the CEO by building and assigning talent, especially key people, and working to unleash the organization's energy. Managing human capital must be accorded the same priority that managing financial capital came to have in the 1980s, when the era of the "super CFO" and serious competitive restructuring began.

CEOs might complain that their CHROs are too bogged down in administrative tasks or that they don't understand the business. But let's be clear: It is up to the CEO to elevate HR and to bridge any gaps that prevent the CHRO from becoming a strategic partner. After all, it was CEOs who boosted the finance function beyond simple accounting. They were also responsible for creating the marketing function from what had been strictly sales.

Elevating HR requires totally redefining the work content of the chief human resources officer—in essence, forging a new contract with this leader—and adopting a new mechanism we call the G3—a core group comprising the CEO, the CFO, and the CHRO. The result will be a CHRO who is as much a value adder as the CFO. Rather than being seen as a supporting player brought in to implement decisions that have already been made, the CHRO will have a central part in corporate decision making and will be properly prepared for that role.

These changes will drive important shifts in career paths for HR executives—and for other leaders across the company. Moreover, the business will benefit from better management of not just its financial resources but also its human ones. We say this with confidence, based on our experience with companies such as General Electric, BlackRock, Tata Communications, and Marsh, all of which act on their commitment to the people side of their businesses.

The CEO's New Contract with the CHRO

A CFO's job is partly defined by the investment community, the board, outside auditors, and regulators. Not so for the CHRO role—that's defined solely by the CEO. The chief executive must have a clear view of the tremendous contribution the CHRO could be making and spell out those expectations in clear, specific language. Putting things in writing ensures that the CEO and CHRO have a shared understanding of appropriate actions and desirable outputs.

To start redefining the job, the CEO should confer with his or her team and key board members, particularly the board's compensation committee (more aptly called the talent and compensation committee), and ask what they expect in an ideal CHRO. Beyond handling the usual HR responsibilities—overseeing employee satisfaction,

Idea in Brief

The Problem

CEOs consistently rank human capital as a top challenge, but they typically undervalue their chief human resources officer and view HR as less important than other functions.

The Solution

The chief human resources officer must become a true strategic partner to the CEO.

The Approach

The CEO must rewrite the CHRO's job description and create a core decision-making body comprising the CEO, CFO, and CHRO.

workforce engagement, benefits and compensation, diversity, and the like—what should an exemplary CHRO do?

Here are three activities we think are critical: predicting outcomes, diagnosing problems, and prescribing actions on the people side that will add value to the business. Some of these things may seem like the usual charter for a CHRO, but they are largely missing in practice, to the disappointment of most CEOs.

Predicting outcomes

CEOs and CFOs normally put together a three-year plan and a one-year budget. The CHRO should be able to assess the chances of meeting the business goals using his knowledge of the people side. How likely is it, for example, that a key group or leader will make timely changes in tune with rapid shifts in the external environment, or that team members will be able to coordinate their efforts? CHROs should raise such questions and offer their views.

Because a company's performance depends largely on the fit between people and jobs, the CHRO can be of enormous help by crystallizing what a particular job requires and realistically assessing whether the assigned person meets those requirements. Jobs that are high leverage require extra attention. Many HR processes tend to treat all employees the same way, but in our observation, 2% of the people in a business drive 98% of the impact. Although coaching can be helpful, particularly when it focuses on one or two things that are preventing individuals from reaching their potential, it has its limits. Nothing overcomes a poor fit. A wide gap between a leader's talents and the job requirements creates problems for the leader, her boss, her peers, and her reports. So before severe damage is done, the CHRO should take the initiative to identify gaps in behavior or skills, especially among those 2% and as job requirements change.

The CHRO, with the CFO, should also consider whether the key performance indicators, talent assignments, and budgets are the right ones to deliver desired outcomes. If necessary, the pair should develop new metrics. Financial information is the most common basis for incentivizing and assessing performance, because it is easy to measure, but the CHRO can propose alternatives. People should be paid according to how much value they contribute to the company—some combination of the importance of the job and how they handle it. Finance and HR should work together to define ahead of time the value that is expected, using qualitative as well as quantitative factors. Imagine the leaders of those functions discussing a business unit manager and triangulating with the CEO and the group executive to better understand what the manager needs to do to outperform the competition in the heat of battle. For example, to move faster into digitization, will he have to reconstitute the team or reallocate funds? Predicting success means weighing how well-attuned the manager is to outside pressures and opportunities, how resilient he would be if the economy went south, and how quickly he could scale up into digitization. The specific metrics would be designed accordingly.

As another example, a top marketing manager might have to build capability for using predictive data in advertising. The CFO and CHRO should recognize that if the manager fails to steep herself in the fundamentals of data analytics and is slow to hire people with that expertise, new competitors could come in and destroy value for the company. Metrics should reflect how quickly the marketing head acts to reorient her department. One set of metrics would focus on the recruiting plan: What steps must the marketing manager take by when? These become milestones to be met at particular points in time. Another set of metrics might focus on budget allocations: Once the new people are hired and assimilated, is the manager real-locating the marketing budget? And is that money in fact helping to increase revenue, margins, market share in selected segments, or brand recognition? Such improvements are measurable, though with a time lag.

The CHRO should also be able to make meaningful predictions about the competition. Just as every army general learns about his counterpart on the enemy side, the CHRO should be armed with information about competitors and how their key decision makers and executors stack up against those at the CHRO's organization. Predictions should include the likely impact of any changes related to human resources at rival companies—such as modifications to their incentive systems, an increase in turnover, or new expertise they are hiring—and what those changes might signify about their market moves. In 2014, for instance, Apple began to hire medi-cal technology people—an early warning sign that it might make a heavy push to use its watch and perhaps other Apple devices for medical purposes. Such activity could have implications for a health care business, a medical device manufacturer, or a clinic. Similarly, a competitor's organizational restructuring and reassignment of leaders might indicate a sharper focus on product lines that could give your company a tougher run.

Intelligence about competitors is often available through head-hunters, the press, employees hired from other companies, suppli-ers, or customers' customers. Even anecdotal information, such as "The marketing VP is a numbers guy, not a people guy," or "She's a cost cutter and can't grow the business," or "The head of their new division comes from a high-growth company," can improve the power of prediction. For example, Motorola might have been able to anticipate the iPhone if the company's CHRO had alerted the CEO when Apple began trying to recruit Motorola's technical people.

The CHRO should make comparisons unit by unit, team by team, and leader by leader, looking not only at established competitors but also at nontraditional ones that could enter the market. Is the person who was promoted to run hair care at X company more experienced and higher-energy than our new division head? Does the development team in charge of wireless sensors at Y company collaborate better than we do? The answers to such questions will help predict outcomes that will show up as numbers on a financial statement sometime in the future.

Diagnosing problems

The CHRO is in a position to pinpoint precisely why an organization might not be performing well or meeting its goals. CEOs must learn to seek such analysis from their CHROs instead of defaulting to consultants.

The CHRO should work with the CEO and CFO to examine the causes of misses, because most problems are people problems. The idea is to look beyond obvious external factors, such as falling interest rates or shifting currency valuations, and to link the numbers with insights into the company's social system—how people work together. A correct diagnosis will suggest the right remedy and avoid any knee-jerk replacements of people who made good decisions but were dealt a bad hand.

If the economy slumped and performance lagged compared to the previous year, the question should be, How did the leader react? Did he get caught like a deer in the headlights or go on the offensive? How fast did he move, relative to the competition and the external change? This is where the CHRO can help make the critical distinction between a leader's misstep and any fundamental unsuitability for the job. Here too the CHRO will learn new things about the leader, such as how resilient he is—information that will be useful in considering future assignments.

But focusing on individual leaders is only half the equation. The CHRO should also be expert at diagnosing how the various parts of the social system are working, systematically looking for activities that are causing bottlenecks or unnecessary friction. When one CEO was reviewing the numbers for an important product line, he saw a decline in market share and profits for the third year in a row. The medical diagnostic product that the group was counting on to reverse the trend was still not ready to launch. As he and his CHRO dug in, they discovered that the marketing team in Milwaukee and the R&D team in France had not agreed on the specifications. On the spot, they arranged a series of face-to-face meetings to resolve the disconnect.

There is great value in having the CHRO diagnose problems and put issues on the table, but such openness is often missing. Behaviors such as withholding information, failing to express disagreement but refusing to take action, and undermining peers often go unnoticed. Some CEOs look the other way rather than tackle conflicts among their direct reports, draining energy and making the whole organization indecisive. Take, for example, problems that arise when collaboration across silos doesn't happen. In such situations, no amount of cost cutting, budget shifting, or admonition will stem the deterioration. Thus CHROs who bring dysfunctional relationships to the surface are worth their weight in gold.

At the same time, the CHRO should watch for employees who are energy creators and develop them. Whether or not they are directly charged with producing results, these are the people who get to the heart of issues, reframe ideas, create informal bonds that encourage collaboration, and in general make the organization healthier and more productive. They may be the hidden power behind the group's value creation.

Prescribing actions to add value

Agile companies know they must move capital to where the opportunities are and not succumb to the all-too-typical imperatives of budgeting inertia ("You get the same funding as last year, plus or minus 5%"). When McKinsey looked at capital allocation patterns in more than 1,600 U.S. companies over 15 years, it found that aggressive reallocators—companies that shifted more than 56% of capital across businesses during that time—had 30% higher total shareholder returns than companies that shifted far less.

Companies should be similarly flexible with their human capital, and CHROs should be prepared to recommend actions that will unlock or create value. These might include recognizing someone's hidden talent and adding that individual to the list of high potentials, moving someone from one position to another to ignite growth in a new market, or bringing in someone from the outside to develop capability in a new technology. Although capital reallocation is important, the reassignment of people along with capital reallocation is what really boosts companies.

Responding to the external environment today sometimes requires leaders with capabilities that weren't previously cultivated, such as knowledge of algorithms, or psychological comfort with digitization and rapid change. The company might have such talent buried at low levels. To have impact, those individuals might need to be lifted three organizational levels at once rather than moved incrementally up existing career ladders. The CHRO should be searching for people who could be future value creators and then thinking imaginatively about how to release their talent. Judging people must be a special skill of the CHRO, just as the CFO has a knack for making inferences from numbers.

Dow Chemical found that aggressively hiring entrepreneurial millennials was the fastest way to create more "short-cycle innovation" alongside the company's traditional long-cycle R&D processes. The share of employees under age 30 went from 9% in 2004 to 15% in 2014. To benefit from this new talent, the company also revamped its career paths to move the 20- and 30-somethings into bigger jobs relatively quickly, and it invited them to global leadership meetings relatively early.

Another way to unlock value is to recommend mechanisms to help an individual bridge a gap or enhance her capacity. These might include moving her to a different job, establishing a council to advise her, or assigning someone to help shore up a particular skill. For example, to build the technology expertise of the small start-ups he funded, the famed venture capitalist John Doerr used his huge relationship network to connect the people running those businesses with top scientists at Bell Labs. In the same vein, CHROs could make better use of their networks with other CHROs to connect people with others who could build their capacity.

The CHRO might also recommend splitting a division into sub-groups to unleash growth and develop more P&L leaders. He might suggest particular skills to look for when hiring a leader to run a country unit or big division. Other prescriptions might focus on improving the social engine—the quality of relationships, the level of trust and collaboration, and decisiveness. The CHRO could, for instance, work with business divisions to conduct reviews once a month rather than annually, because reducing the time lag between actions and feedback increases motivation and improves operations.

What not to do

In addition to spelling out clearly what is expected in the way of making predictions, diagnosing problems, and prescribing beneficial actions, the CHRO's new contract should define what she is *not* required to do. This helps provide focus and free time so that she can engage at a higher level. For example, the transactional and administrative work of HR, including managing benefits, could be cordoned off and reassigned, as some companies have begun to do. One option is to give those responsibilities to the CFO. At Netflix, traditional HR processes and routines are organized under the finance function, while HR serves only as a talent scout and coach. Another model we see emerging is to create a shared service function that combines the back-office activities of HR, finance, and IT. This function may or may not report to the CFO.

Compensation has traditionally been the purview of CHROs, but it may be hard for them to appreciate the specific issues business leaders face, just as it is hard for the CFO to understand the nuances of the social engine. Because compensation has such an enormous impact on behavior and on the speed and agility of the corporation, the best solution is for the CEO and CFO to also get involved. While the CHRO can be the lead dog, compensation decisions should be made jointly by the three—and, given the increasingly active role of institutional investors, with the board's engagement.

The CHRO's fit

With a new contract in hand, the chief executive should assess how well the CHRO meets the job specifications now and where he needs to be in three years. Most CHROs have come up through the HR pipeline. While some have had line jobs, most have not; Korn Ferry research indicates that only 40 of the CHROs at *Fortune* 100 companies had significant work experience outside HR before they came to lead that function. This might leave a gap in terms of predicting, diagnosing, and prescribing actions that will improve business performance. However, inclusion in broader discussions will expand a CHRO's understanding of the business. CEOs should give their CHRO a chance to grow into the newly defined role, and they should assess progress quarter by quarter.

Measuring the performance of the CHRO has long been problematic. HR leaders are usually judged on accomplishments such as installing a new process under budget, recruiting a targeted number of people from the right places, or improving retention or employee engagement. Yet such efforts are not directly tied to value creation. In keeping with recasting HR as a value creator rather than a cost center, performance should be measured by outputs that are more closely linked to revenue, profit margin, brand recognition, or market share. And the closer the linkage, the better.

A CHRO can add value by, for example, moving a key person from one boss to another and improving his performance; arranging for coaching that strengthens a crucial skill; bringing a person from the outside into a pivotal position; putting two or three people together to create a new business or initiative to grow the top or bottom line; reassigning a division manager because she will not be able to meet the challenge two years out; or discovering and smoothing friction where collaboration is required. Such actions are observable, verifiable, and closely related to the company's performance and numbers.

Here's a case in point: When a promising young leader was put in charge of three divisions of a large company, replacing an executive vice president with long tenure, the divisions took off. The new EVP, who was growth-oriented and digitally savvy, seized on commonalities among the three businesses in technology and production and nearly halved the product development cycle time. In three years the divisions overtook the competition to become number one.

Creating a G3

To make the CHRO a true partner, the CEO should create a triumvirate at the top of the corporation that includes both the CFO and the CHRO. Forming such a team is the single best way to link financial numbers with the people who produce them. It also signals to the organization that you are lifting HR into the inner sanctum and that the CHRO's contribution will be analogous to the CFO's. Although some companies may want the CHRO to be part of an expanded group that includes, say, a chief technology officer or chief risk officer, the G3, as we call it, is the core group that should steer the company, and it should meet apart from everyone else. The G3 will shape the destiny of the business by looking forward and at the big picture while others bury their heads in operations, and it will ensure that the company stays on the rails by homing in on any problems in execution. It is the G3 that makes the connection between the organization and business results.

At Marsh, a global leader in insurance brokerage and risk management, CEO Peter Zaffino often has one-on-one discussions with his CFO, Courtney Leimkuhler, and his CHRO, Mary Anne Elliott. In April 2015 he held a meeting with both of them to assess the alignment of the organization with desired business outcomes. The G3 began this meeting by selecting a business in the portfolio and drawing a vertical line down the middle of a blank page on a flip chart. The right side was for the business performance (Leimkuhler's expertise); the left side for organizational design issues (Elliott's expertise). A horizontal line created boxes for the answers to two simple questions: What is going well? What is not going well?

"Peter could have filled in the entire two-by-two chart on his own," Elliott says, "but doing it together really added value." Zaffino adds, "The whole meeting took about 15 minutes. We found the exercise to be very worthwhile. We already run the business with disciplined processes. We conduct deep dives into the organization's financial performance through quarterly operational reviews, and we conduct quarterly talent reviews, where we focus on the human capital side. So you might not think we'd want to introduce another process to evaluate how we are managing the business. But this G3 process provided us with a terrific lens into the business without adding bureaucracy."

Working together to synthesize disparate data points into one flip chart helped the team identify items on the organizational side that would predict business performance in the next four to eight quarters. Significant value came from the dialogue as connections emerged naturally. Zaffino says, "We constantly drill down deep to understand why a business is performing the way it is. In those instances, we are drilling vertically, not horizontally, when there could be some items identified on the organizational side that are actually driving the performance." Zaffino cited the implementation of a new sales plan, which HR was working on, as one example. His concern was making sure business results were aligned with remuneration "so we didn't have sales compensation becoming disconnected from the overall financial result of the business," he explains. "We also didn't want to drive top-line growth without knowing how to invest back in the business and increase profitability." The CHRO was thinking it through from her perspective: Is this sales plan motivating the right behaviors so that it moves business performance to the "going well" category?

Seeing the interconnections also helped the trio identify what mattered most. "It's easy enough to list everything we want to do better," Leimkuhler says, "but it's hard to know where to start. When you understand which things on the organizational side are really advancing business performance, it makes it easier to prioritize." For example, managing the transition of regional business leaders was a big issue for HR—one that, because of its difficulty, would have been easy to push off. Seeing the extent to which inaction could be holding back business performance created a greater sense of urgency.

"In the HR world, we talk about understanding and integrating with the business," Elliott notes. "G3 meetings are a pragmatic activity. When you're sitting with the CEO and CFO, there's no place for academic HR. It's all about understanding what the organization needs to do to drive business performance and how to align those key variables."

"There's something to be said for peeling off into a smaller group," Leimkuhler adds. "It would be unwieldy to have this discussion with the full executive committee, which at Marsh consists of 10 executives. In any case, it's not one or the other; it's additive." Says Zaffino, "This was a streamlined way to get a holistic view of the business. Each of us left the first G3 meeting feeling comfortable that the organization and the business were aligned and that we have a very good handle on the business."

Vinod Kumar, CEO of Tata Communications, also uses an informal G3 mechanism. Kumar's company supplies communication, computing, and collaboration infrastructure to large global companies, including many telephone and mobile operators. In 2012 there were price drops of 15% to 20%, and disruptive technologies were par for the course. To keep pace, Tata Communications had to transform its business very quickly, which meant building critical new capabilities by hiring from the outside, at least in the short term—an effort that would hardly help the company deal with rising costs. Something had to give, and Kumar enlisted then-CFO Sanjay Baweja and CHRO Aadesh Goyal to help chart a path forward while taking into account both financial and talent considerations.

Frequent discussions among the G3 led to a consensus: Tata Communications would restructure roles that had become redundant or were out of sync with the company's new direction, and it would move jobs to the right geographical locations. These actions would reduce staffing costs by 7%. The company would use the savings to build the necessary capabilities, mainly by making new hires, especially in sales, marketing, and technology.

The G3 next went to work on changes that would occur over a longer time. Tata Communications launched a companywide program in late 2013 aimed at continuously improving productivity. The initial objective was to reduce the cost base by $100 million, but the overall intention was to seed a new culture. The G3 began by creating a cross-functional team that employees joined part-time. Ultimately more than 500 people participated, working on ideas in

50 categories and achieving even more cost reductions than originally targeted. In short, the project was a big success, and it continues to produce results.

Dialogue—both institutionalized and informal—between the CHRO, the CFO, and the CEO is now a way of life at Tata Communications. In time, as CHRO Goyal's grasp of the business became evident, Kumar made a bold move: He gave Goyal the additional responsibility of managing one of the company's high-growth subsidiaries and made him part of the Innovation Council, which identifies opportunities to invest in and incubate new businesses.

Regular G3 Meetings

If a G3 is to be effective, the CEO has to ensure that the triumvirate meets on a regular basis.

Weekly temperature taking

The CEO, CFO, and CHRO should get together once a week to discuss any early warning signals they are picking up internally or externally about the condition of the social engine. Each of them will see things through a different lens, and pooling their thoughts will yield a more accurate picture. The three don't have to be together physically—they can arrange a conference call or video chat—but meeting frequently is important. After about six weeks, and with discipline, such sessions could be finished in 15 to 20 minutes.

The CEO has to set the tone for these reviews, ensuring that the discussion is balanced and that intellectual honesty and integrity are absolute. It's a given that both the CFO and the CHRO must be politically neutral to build trust, and they must never sacrifice their integrity to be the CEO's henchmen. They must be willing to speak up and tell it like it is. Over time, each G3 member will have a better understanding of the others' cognitive lenses, discussions will be more fluid, and all three will learn a lot about the intricacies of the business. They will also become more comfortable correcting one another's biases, more skilled at reading people, and more likely to get the right people in the right jobs.

Looking forward monthly

The G3 should spend a couple of hours every month looking four and eight quarters ahead with these questions in mind: What people issues would prevent us from meeting our goals? Is there a problem with an individual? With collaboration? Is a senior team member unable to see how the competition is moving? Is somebody likely to leave us?

Companies do operational reviews, which are backward-looking, at least quarterly. The objective here is to be predictive and diagnostic, looking forward not just at the numbers but also at the people side, because most failures and missed opportunities are people-related. There may be organizational issues, energy drains, or conflicts among silos, particularly in the top two layers. Conflicts are inherent in matrix organizations; the G3 needs to know where they exist, whether they could affect progress on a new initiative, and how the leaders in charge are handling them. Probing such matters is not micromanagement or a witch hunt. It's a means of finding the real causes of both good and poor performance and taking corrective action promptly or preemptively.

Planning three years out

It is common practice to plan where the company needs to be in three years and to decide what new projects to fund and where to invest capital. Often missing from that process is exploration of the people questions: Will we have employees with the right skills, training, and temperament to achieve the targets? Will our people have the flexibility to adapt to changing circumstances? In most strategic planning, there is zero consideration of the critical players in the organization—or those working for competitors.

Discussion of people should come before discussion of strategy. (This is a practice that General Electric is known for.) What are employees' capabilities, what help might they need, and are they the very best? The CEO and the CHRO of one company decided that for every high-leverage position that opened, they should have five candidates—three from inside, two from outside. Talent should always be viewed in a broad context. Consider who is excelling, being let go, or being lured away, along with any other information that could affect your competitiveness or your rivals'.

New HR Leadership Channels

Some CEOs might be holding back on elevating their CHROs because they lack confidence in the HR leader's business judgment and people acumen. There's a fear that HR chiefs aren't prepared to discuss issues beyond hiring, firing, payroll, benefits, and the like. That reservation must be met head-on by providing rich opportunities for CHROs to learn. Give them more exposure to the business side through meetings of the G3, and provide some coaching. If knowledge or skills gaps persist, ask the CHRO how she might fill them. Some CHROs will rise to the occasion. Others won't measure up, and the supply of suitable replacements might be scarce at first. (The same issue applied in the 1980s to finding the right CFO types from the ranks of accounting.)

An enduring solution is to create new career paths for HR leaders to cultivate business smarts and for business leaders to cultivate people smarts. Every entry-level leader, whether in HR or some other job, should get rigorous training in judging, recruiting, and coaching people. And those who begin their careers in HR leadership should go through rigorous training in business analysis, along the lines of what McKinsey requires for all its new recruits. There should be no straight-line leadership promotions up the functional HR silo. Aspiring CHROs should have line jobs along the way, where they have to manage people and budgets.

All leaders headed for top jobs should alternate between positions in HR and in the rest of the business. Make it a requirement for people in the top three layers of the company to have successfully worked as an HR leader, and the function will soon become a talent magnet. Be sure that it isn't just ticket punching. Those who have no feel for the people side are unlikely to succeed for long in high-level jobs.

The Transition to the New HR

Any CEO who is sold on the idea that people are the ultimate source of sustainable competitive differentiation must take the rejuvenation and elevation of the HR function very seriously. Creating a mechanism that knits the CFO and the CHRO together will improve the business and expand the CEO's personal capability. It won't happen overnight—three years seems to us the minimum time required to achieve a shift of this magnitude. Stating the new expectations for the CHRO and the human resources function is a good place to begin. Creating ways to blend business and people acumen should follow. And redesigning career tracks and talent reviews will take the company further still. But none of this will happen unless the CEO personally embraces the challenge, makes a three-year commitment, and starts executing.

Originally published in July–August 2015. Reprint R1507D

How Netflix Reinvented HR

by Patty McCord

SHERYL SANDBERG HAS CALLED it one of the most important documents ever to come out of Silicon Valley. It's been viewed more than 5 million times on the web. But when Reed Hastings and I (along with some colleagues) wrote a PowerPoint deck explaining how we shaped the culture and motivated performance at Netflix, where Hastings is CEO and I was chief talent officer from 1998 to 2012, we had no idea it would go viral. We realized that some of the talent management ideas we'd pioneered, such as the concept that workers should be allowed to take whatever vacation time they feel is appropriate, had been seen as a little crazy (at least until other companies started adopting them). But we were surprised that an unadorned set of 127 slides—no music, no animation—would become so influential.

People find the Netflix approach to talent and culture compelling for a few reasons. The most obvious one is that Netflix has been really successful: During 2013 alone its stock more than tripled, it won three Emmy awards, and its U.S. subscriber base grew to nearly 29 million. All that aside, the approach is compelling because it derives from common sense. In this article I'll go beyond the bullet points to describe five ideas that have defined the way Netflix attracts, retains, and manages talent. But first I'll share two conversations I had with early employees, both of which helped shape our overall philosophy.

The first took place in late 2001. Netflix had been growing quickly: We'd reached about 120 employees and had been planning an IPO. But after the dot-com bubble burst and the 9/11 attacks occurred, things changed. It became clear that we needed to put the IPO on hold and lay off a third of our employees. It was brutal. Then, a bit unexpectedly, DVD players became the hot gift that Christmas. By early 2002 our DVD-by-mail subscription business was growing like crazy. Suddenly we had far more work to do, with 30% fewer employees.

One day I was talking with one of our best engineers, an employee I'll call John. Before the layoffs, he'd managed three engineers, but now he was a one-man department working very long hours. I told John I hoped to hire some help for him soon. His response surprised me. "There's no rush—I'm happier now," he said. It turned out that the engineers we'd laid off weren't spectacular—they were merely adequate. John realized that he'd spent too much time riding herd on them and fixing their mistakes. "I've learned that I'd rather work by myself than with subpar performers," he said. His words echo in my mind whenever I describe the most basic element of Netflix's talent philosophy: The best thing you can do for employees—a perk better than foosball or free sushi—is hire only "A" players to work alongside them. Excellent colleagues trump everything else.

The second conversation took place in 2002, a few months after our IPO. Laura, our bookkeeper, was bright, hardworking, and creative. She'd been very important to our early growth, having devised a system for accurately tracking movie rentals so that we could pay the correct royalties. But now, as a public company, we needed CPAs and other fully credentialed, deeply experienced accounting professionals—and Laura had only an associate's degree from a community college. Despite her work ethic, her track record, and the fact that we all really liked her, her skills were no longer adequate. Some of us talked about jury-rigging a new role for her, but we decided that wouldn't be right.

So I sat down with Laura and explained the situation—and said that in light of her spectacular service, we would give her a spectacular severance package. I'd braced myself for tears or histrionics, but

Idea in Brief

The Idea

If a company hires correctly, workers will want to be star performers, and they can be managed through honest communication and common sense. Most companies focus too much on formal policies aimed at the small number of employees whose interests *aren't* fully aligned with the firm's.

The Solution

Hire, reward, and tolerate only fully formed adults. Tell the truth about performance. Make clear to managers that their top priority is building great teams. Leaders should create the company culture, and talent managers should think like innovative businesspeople and not fall into the traditional HR mind-set.

Laura reacted well: She was sad to be leaving but recognized that the generous severance would let her regroup, retrain, and find a new career path. This incident helped us create the other vital element of our talent management philosophy: If we wanted only "A" players on our team, we had to be willing to let go of people whose skills no longer fit, no matter how valuable their contributions had once been. Out of fairness to such people—and, frankly, to help us overcome our discomfort with discharging them—we learned to offer rich severance packages.

With these two overarching principles in mind, we shaped our approach to talent using the five tenets below.

Hire, Reward, and Tolerate Only Fully Formed Adults

Over the years we learned that if we asked people to rely on logic and common sense instead of on formal policies, most of the time we would get better results, and at lower cost. If you're careful to hire people who will put the company's interests first, who understand and support the desire for a high-performance workplace, 97% of your employees will do the right thing. Most companies spend endless time and money writing and enforcing HR policies to deal with problems the other 3% might cause. Instead, we tried really hard to not hire those people, and we let them go if it turned out we'd made a hiring mistake.

Adultlike behavior means talking openly about issues with your boss, your colleagues, and your subordinates. It means recognizing that even in companies with reams of HR policies, those policies are frequently skirted as managers and their reports work out what makes sense on a case-by-case basis.

Let me offer two examples.

When Netflix launched, we had a standard paid-time-off policy: People got 10 vacation days, 10 holidays, and a few sick days. We used an honor system—employees kept track of the days they took off and let their managers know when they'd be out. After we went public, our auditors freaked. They said Sarbanes-Oxley mandated that we account for time off. We considered instituting a formal tracking system. But then Reed asked, "Are companies *required* to give time off? If not, can't we just handle it informally and skip the accounting rigmarole?" I did some research and found that, indeed, no California law governed vacation time.

So instead of shifting to a formal system, we went in the opposite direction: Salaried employees were told to take whatever time they felt was appropriate. Bosses and employees were asked to work it out with one another. (Hourly workers in call centers and warehouses were given a more structured policy.) We did provide some guidance. If you worked in accounting or finance, you shouldn't plan to be out during the beginning or the end of a quarter, because those were busy times. If you wanted 30 days off in a row, you needed to meet with HR. Senior leaders were urged to take vacations and to let people know about them—they were role models for the policy. (Most were happy to comply.) Some people worried about whether the system would be inconsistent—whether some bosses would allow tons of time off while others would be stingy. In general, I worried more about fairness than consistency, because the reality is that in any organization, the highest-performing and most valuable employees get more leeway.

We also departed from a formal travel and expense policy and decided to simply require adultlike behavior there, too. The company's expense policy is five words long: "Act in Netflix's best interests." In talking that through with employees, we said we expected them to spend company money frugally, as if it were their own. Eliminating a formal policy and forgoing expense account police shifted responsibility to frontline managers, where it belongs. It also reduced costs: Many large companies still use travel agents (and pay their fees) to book trips, as a way to enforce travel policies. They could save money by letting employees book their own trips online. Like most Netflix managers, I had to have conversations periodically with employees who ate at lavish restaurants (meals that would have been fine for sales or recruiting, but not for eating alone or with a Netflix colleague). We kept an eye on our IT guys, who were prone to buying a lot of gadgets. But overall we found that expense accounts are another area where if you create a clear expectation of responsible behavior, most employees will comply.

Tell the Truth About Performance

Many years ago we eliminated formal reviews. We had held them for a while but came to realize they didn't make sense—they were too ritualistic and too infrequent. So we asked managers and employees to have conversations about performance as an organic part of their work. In many functions—sales, engineering, product development—it's fairly obvious how well people are doing. (As companies develop better analytics to measure performance, this becomes even truer.) Building a bureaucracy and elaborate rituals around measuring performance usually doesn't improve it.

Traditional corporate performance reviews are driven largely by fear of litigation. The theory is that if you want to get rid of someone, you need a paper trail documenting a history of poor achievement. At many companies, low performers are placed on "Performance Improvement Plans." I detest PIPs. I think they're fundamentally dishonest: They never accomplish what their name implies.

One Netflix manager requested a PIP for a quality assurance engineer named Maria, who had been hired to help develop our streaming service. The technology was new, and it was evolving very quickly. Maria's job was to find bugs. She was fast, intuitive, and hardworking. But in time we figured out how to automate the QA tests. Maria didn't like automation and wasn't particularly good at it. Her new boss (brought in to create a world-class automation tools team) told me he wanted to start a PIP with her.

I replied, "Why bother? We know how this will play out. You'll write up objectives and deliverables for her to achieve, which she can't, because she lacks the skills. Every Wednesday you'll take time away from your real work to discuss (and document) her shortcomings. You won't sleep on Tuesday nights, because you'll know it will be an awful meeting, and the same will be true for her. After a few weeks there will be tears. This will go on for three months. The entire team will know. And at the end you'll fire her. None of this will make any sense to her, because for five years she's been consistently rewarded for being great at her job—a job that basically doesn't exist anymore. Tell me again how Netflix benefits?

"Instead, let's just tell the truth: Technology has changed, the company has changed, and Maria's skills no longer apply. This won't be a surprise to her: She's been in the trenches, watching the work around her shift. Give her a great severance package—which, when she signs the documents, will dramatically reduce (if not eliminate) the chance of a lawsuit." In my experience, people can handle anything as long as they're told the truth—and this proved to be the case with Maria.

When we stopped doing formal performance reviews, we instituted informal 360-degree reviews. We kept them fairly simple: People were asked to identify things that colleagues should stop, start, or continue. In the beginning we used an anonymous software system, but over time we shifted to signed feedback, and many teams held their 360s face-to-face.

HR people can't believe that a company the size of Netflix doesn't hold annual reviews. "Are you making this up just to upset us?" they ask. I'm not. If you talk simply and honestly about performance on a regular basis, you can get good results—probably better ones than a company that grades everyone on a five-point scale.

Crafting a Culture of Excellence

NETFLIX FOUNDER AND CEO Reed Hastings discusses the company's unconventional HR practices.

HBR: Why did you write the Netflix culture deck?

Hastings: It's our version of *Letters to a Young Poet* for budding entrepreneurs. It's what we wish we had understood when we started. More than 100 people at Netflix have made major contributions to the deck, and we have more improvements coming.

Many of the ideas in it seem like common sense, but they go against traditional HR practices. Why aren't companies more innovative when it comes to talent management?

As a society, we've had hundreds of years to work on managing industrial firms, so a lot of accepted HR practices are centered in that experience. We're just beginning to learn how to run creative firms, which is quite different. Industrial firms thrive on reducing variation (manufacturing errors); creative firms thrive on *increasing* variation (innovation).

What reactions have you gotten from your peers to steps such as abolishing formal vacation and performance review policies? In general, do you think other companies admire your HR innovations or look askance at them?

My peers are mostly in the creative sector, and many of the ideas in our culture deck came from them. We are all learning from one another.

Which idea in the culture deck was the hardest sell with employees?

"Adequate performance gets a generous severance package." It's a pretty blunt statement of our hunger for excellence.

Have any of your talent management innovations been total flops?

Not so far.

Patty talks about how leaders should model appropriate behaviors to help people adapt to an environment with fewer formal controls. With that in mind, how many days off did you take in 2013?

"Days off" is a very industrial concept, like being "at the office." I find Netflix fun to think about, so there are probably no 24-hour periods when I never think about work. But I did take three or four weeklong family trips over the past year, which were both stimulating and relaxing.

Managers Own the Job of Creating Great Teams

Discussing the military's performance during the Iraq War, Donald Rumsfeld, the former defense secretary, once famously said, "You go to war with the army you have, not the army you might want or wish to have at a later time." When I talk to managers about creating great teams, I tell them to approach the process in exactly the opposite way.

In my consulting work, I ask managers to imagine a documentary about what their team is accomplishing six months from now. What specific results do they see? How is the work different from what the team is doing today? Next I ask them to think about the skills needed to make the images in the movie become reality. Nowhere in the early stages of the process do I advise them to think about the team they actually have. Only after they've done the work of envisioning the ideal outcome and the skill set necessary to achieve it should they analyze how well their existing team matches what they need.

If you're in a fast-changing business environment, you're probably looking at a lot of mismatches. In that case, you need to have honest conversations about letting some team members find a place where their skills are a better fit. You also need to recruit people with the right skills.

We faced the latter challenge at Netflix in a fairly dramatic way as we began to shift from DVDs by mail to a streaming service. We had to store massive volumes of files in the cloud and figure out how huge numbers of people could reliably access them. (By some estimates, up to a third of peak residential internet traffic in the U.S. comes from customers streaming Netflix movies.) So we needed to find people deeply experienced with cloud services who worked for companies that operate on a giant scale—companies like Amazon, eBay, Google, and Facebook, which aren't the easiest places to hire someone away from.

Our compensation philosophy helped a lot. Most of its principles stem from ideals described earlier: Be honest, and treat people like adults. For instance, during my tenure Netflix didn't pay performance bonuses, because we believed that they're unnecessary if you hire the right people. If your employees are fully formed adults who put the company first, an annual bonus won't make them work harder or smarter. We also believed in market-based pay and would tell employees that it was smart to interview with competitors when they had the chance, in order to get a good sense of the market rate for their talent. Many HR people dislike it when employees talk to recruiters, but I always told employees to take the call, ask how much, and send me the number—it's valuable information.

In addition, we used equity compensation much differently from the way most companies do. Instead of larding stock options on top of a competitive salary, we let employees choose how much (if any) of their compensation would be in the form of equity. If employees wanted stock options, we reduced their salaries accordingly. We believed that they were sophisticated enough to understand the trade-offs, judge their personal tolerance for risk, and decide what was best for them and their families. We distributed options every month, at a slight discount from the market price. We had no vesting period—the options could be cashed in immediately. Most tech companies have a four-year vesting schedule and try to use options as "golden handcuffs" to aid retention, but we never thought that made sense. If you see a better opportunity elsewhere, you should be allowed to take what you've earned and leave. If you no longer want to work with us, we don't want to hold you hostage.

We continually told managers that building a great team was their most important task. We didn't measure them on whether they were excellent coaches or mentors or got their paperwork done on time. Great teams accomplish great work, and recruiting the right team was the top priority.

Leaders Own the Job of Creating the Company Culture

After I left Netflix and began consulting, I visited a hot start-up in San Francisco. It had 60 employees in an open loft-style office with a foosball table, two pool tables, and a kitchen, where a chef cooked lunch for the entire staff. As the CEO showed me around, he talked about creating a fun atmosphere. At one point I asked him what the most important value for his company was. He replied, "Efficiency."

"OK," I said. "Imagine that I work here, and it's 2:58 p.m. I'm playing an intense game of pool, and I'm winning. I estimate that I can finish the game in five minutes. We have a meeting at 3:00. Should I stay and win the game or cut it short for the meeting?"

"You should finish the game," he insisted. I wasn't surprised; like many tech start-ups, this was a casual place, where employees wore hoodies and brought pets to work, and that kind of casualness often extends to punctuality. "Wait a second," I said. "You told me that efficiency is your most important cultural value. It's not efficient to delay a meeting and keep coworkers waiting because of a pool game. Isn't there a mismatch between the values you're talking up and the behaviors you're modeling and encouraging?"

When I advise leaders about molding a corporate culture, I tend to see three issues that need attention. This type of mismatch is one. It's a particular problem at start-ups, where there's a premium on casualness that can run counter to the high-performance ethos leaders want to create. I often sit in on company meetings to get a sense of how people operate. I frequently see CEOs who are clearly winging it. They lack a real agenda. They're working from slides that were obviously put together an hour before or were recycled from the previous round of VC meetings. Workers notice these things, and if they see a leader who's not fully prepared and who relies on charm, IQ, and improvisation, it affects how they perform, too. It's a waste of time to articulate ideas about values and culture if you don't model and reward behavior that aligns with those goals.

The second issue has to do with making sure employees understand the levers that drive the business. I recently visited a Texas start-up whose employees were mostly engineers in their twenties. "I bet half the people in this room have never read a P&L," I said to the CFO. He replied, "It's true—they're not financially savvy or business savvy, and our biggest challenge is teaching them how the business works." Even if you've hired people who want to perform well, you need to clearly communicate how the company makes money and what behaviors will drive its success. At Netflix, for instance, employees used to focus too heavily on subscriber growth, without much awareness that our expenses often ran ahead of it: We were spending huge amounts buying DVDs, setting up distribution centers, and ordering original programming, all before we'd collected a cent from our new subscribers. Our employees needed to learn that even though revenue was growing, managing expenses really mattered.

The third issue is something I call the split personality start-up. At tech companies this usually manifests itself as a schism between the engineers and the sales team, but it can take other forms. At Netflix, for instance, I sometimes had to remind people that there were big differences between the salaried professional staff at headquarters and the hourly workers in the call centers. At one point our finance team wanted to shift the whole company to direct-deposit paychecks, and I had to point out that some of our hourly workers didn't have bank accounts. That's a small example, but it speaks to a larger point: As leaders build a company culture, they need to be aware of subcultures that might require different management.

Good Talent Managers Think Like Businesspeople and Innovators First, and Like HR People Last

Throughout most of my career I've belonged to professional associations of human resources executives. Although I like the people in these groups personally, I often find myself disagreeing with them. Too many devote time to morale improvement initiatives. At some places entire teams focus on getting their firm onto lists of "Best Places to Work" (which, when you dig into the methodologies, are really based just on perks and benefits). At a recent conference I met someone from a company that had appointed a "chief happiness officer"—a concept that makes me slightly sick.

During 30 years in business I've never seen an HR initiative that improved morale. HR departments might throw parties and hand out T-shirts, but if the stock price is falling or the company's products aren't perceived as successful, the people at those parties will quietly complain—and they'll use the T-shirts to wash their cars.

Instead of cheerleading, people in my profession should think of themselves as businesspeople. What's good for the company? How do we communicate that to employees? How can we help every worker understand what we mean by high performance?

Here's a simple test: If your company has a performance bonus plan, go up to a random employee and ask, "Do you know specifically what you should be doing right now to increase your bonus?" If he or she can't answer, the HR team isn't making things as clear as they need to be.

At Netflix I worked with colleagues who were changing the way people consume filmed entertainment, which is an incredibly innovative pursuit—yet when I started there, the expectation was that I would default to mimicking other companies' best practices (many of them antiquated), which is how almost everyone seems to approach HR. I rejected those constraints. There's no reason the HR team can't be innovative too.

Originally published in January–February 2014. **Reprint** R1401E

HR Goes Agile

by Peter Cappelli and Anna Tavis

AGILE ISN'T JUST FOR TECH anymore. It's been working its way into other areas and functions, from product development to manufacturing to marketing—and now it's transforming how organizations hire, develop, and manage their people.

You could say HR is going "agile lite," applying the general principles without adopting all the tools and protocols from the tech world. It's a move away from a rules- and planning-based approach toward a simpler and faster model driven by feedback from participants. This new paradigm has really taken off in the area of performance management. (In a 2017 Deloitte survey, 79% of global executives rated agile performance management as a high organizational priority.) But other HR processes are starting to change too.

In many companies that's happening gradually, almost organically, as a spillover from IT, where more than 90% of organizations already use agile practices. At the Bank of Montreal (BMO), for example, the shift began as tech employees joined cross-functional product-development teams to make the bank more customer focused. The business side has learned agile principles from IT colleagues, and IT has learned about customer needs from the business. One result is that BMO now thinks about performance management in terms of teams, not just individuals. Elsewhere the move to agile HR has been faster and more deliberate. GE is a prime example. Seen for many years as a paragon of management through control systems, it switched to Fast-Works, a lean approach that cuts back on top-down financial controls and empowers teams to manage projects as needs evolve.

The changes in HR have been a long time coming. After World War II, when manufacturing dominated the industrial landscape, planning was at the heart of human resources: Companies recruited lifers, gave them rotational assignments to support their development, groomed them years in advance to take on bigger and bigger roles, and tied their raises directly to each incremental move up the ladder. The bureaucracy was the point: Organizations wanted their talent practices to be rules-based and internally consistent so that they could reliably meet five-year (and sometimes 15-year) plans. That made sense. Every other aspect of companies, from core businesses to administrative functions, took the long view in their goal setting, budgeting, and operations. HR reflected and supported what they were doing.

By the 1990s, as business became less predictable and companies needed to acquire new skills fast, that traditional approach began to bend—but it didn't quite break. Lateral hiring from the outside—to get more flexibility—replaced a good deal of the internal development and promotions. "Broadband" compensation gave managers greater latitude to reward people for growth and achievement within roles. For the most part, though, the old model persisted. Like other functions, HR was still built around the long term. Workforce and succession planning carried on, even though changes in the economy and in the business often rendered those plans irrelevant. Annual appraisals continued, despite almost universal dissatisfaction with them.

Now we're seeing a more sweeping transformation. Why is this the moment for it? Because rapid innovation has become a strategic imperative for most companies, not just a subset. To get it, businesses have looked to Silicon Valley and to software companies in particular, emulating their agile practices for managing projects. So top-down planning models are giving way to nimbler, user-driven methods that are better suited for adapting in the near term, such as rapid prototyping, iterative feedback, team-based decisions, and task-centered "sprints." As BMO's chief transformation officer, Lynn Roger, puts it, "Speed is the new business currency."

Idea in Brief

The Reason for the Shift

Companies' core businesses and functions have largely replaced long-range planning models with nimbler methods that allow them to adapt and innovate more quickly. HR is starting to use agile talent practices to reflect and support what the rest of the organization is doing.

The Areas of Transformation

Organizations are radically changing how they manage performance and evaluate talent, what skills they emphasize and develop, how they approach recruitment and rewards, and what they do to facilitate learning.

With the business justification for the old HR systems gone and the agile playbook available to copy, people management is finally getting its long-awaited overhaul too. In this article we'll illustrate some of the profound changes companies are making in their talent practices and describe the challenges they face in their transition to agile HR.

Where We're Seeing the Biggest Changes

Because HR touches every aspect—and every employee—of an organization, its agile transformation may be even more extensive (and more difficult) than the changes in other functions. Companies are redesigning their talent practices in the following areas:

Performance appraisals

When businesses adopted agile methods in their core operations, they dropped the charade of trying to plan a year or more in advance how projects would go and when they would end. So in many cases the first traditional HR practice to go was the annual performance review, along with employee goals that "cascaded" down from business and unit objectives each year. As individuals worked on shorter-term projects of various lengths, often run by different leaders and organized around teams, the notion that performance feedback would come once a year, from one boss, made little sense. They needed more of it, more often, from more people.

An early-days CEB survey suggested that people actually got *less* feedback and support when their employers dropped annual reviews. However, that's because many companies put nothing in their place. Managers felt no pressing need to adopt a new feedback model and shifted their attention to other priorities. But dropping appraisals without a plan to fill the void was of course a recipe for failure.

Since learning that hard lesson, many organizations have switched to frequent performance assessments, often conducted project by project. This change has spread to a number of industries, including retail (Gap), big pharma (Pfizer), insurance (Cigna), investing (OppenheimerFunds), consumer products (P&G), and accounting (all Big Four firms). It is most famous at GE, across the firm's range of businesses, and at IBM. Overall, the focus is on delivering more-immediate feedback throughout the year so that teams can become nimbler, "course-correct" mistakes, improve performance, and learn through iteration—all key agile principles.

In user-centered fashion, managers and employees have had a hand in shaping, testing, and refining new processes. For instance, Johnson & Johnson offered its businesses the chance to participate in an experiment: They could try out a new continual-feedback process, using a customized app with which employees, peers, and bosses could exchange comments in real time.

The new process was an attempt to move away from J&J's event-driven "five conversations" framework (which focused on goal setting, career discussion, a midyear performance review, a year-end appraisal, and a compensation review) and toward a model of ongoing dialogue. Those who tried it were asked to share how well everything worked, what the bugs were, and so on. The experiment lasted three months. At first only 20% of the managers in the pilot actively participated. The inertia from prior years of annual appraisals was hard to overcome. But then the company used training to show managers what good feedback could look like and designated "change champions" to model the desired behaviors on their teams. By the end of the three months, 46% of managers in the pilot group had joined in, exchanging 3,000 pieces of feedback.

Why Intuit's Transition to Agile Almost Stalled Out

THE FINANCIAL SERVICES DIVISION at Intuit began shifting to agile in 2009—but four years went by before that became standard operating procedure across the company.

What took so long? Leaders started with a "waterfall" approach to change management, because that's what they knew best. It didn't work. Spotty support from middle management, part-time commitments to the team leading the transformation, scarce administrative resources, and an extended planning cycle all put a big drag on the rollout.

Before agile could gain traction throughout the organization, the transition team needed to take an agile approach to *becoming* agile and managing the change. Looking back, Joumana Youssef, one of Intuit's strategic-change leaders, identifies several critical discoveries that changed the course—and the speed—of the transformation:

- Focus on early adopters. Don't waste time trying to convert naysayers.

- Form "triple-S" (small, stable, self-managed) teams, give them ownership of their work, and hold them accountable for their commitments.

- Quickly train leaders at all levels in agile methods. Agile teams need to be fully supported to self-manage.

- Expect that changing frontline and middle management will be hard, because people in those roles need time to acclimate to "servant leadership," which is primarily about coaching and supporting employees rather than monitoring them.

- Stay the course. Even though agile change is faster than a waterfall approach, shifting your organization's mindset takes persistence.

Regeneron Pharmaceuticals, a fast-growing biotech company, is going even further with its appraisals overhaul. Michelle Weitzman-Garcia, Regeneron's head of workforce development, argued that the performance of the scientists working on drug development, the product supply group, the field sales force, and the corporate functions should not be measured on the same cycle or in the same way. She observed that these employee groups needed varying feedback and that they even operated on different calendars.

So the company created four distinct appraisal processes, tailored to the various groups' needs. The research scientists and postdocs, for example, crave metrics and are keen on assessing competencies, so they meet with managers twice a year for competency evaluations and milestones reviews. Customer-facing groups include feedback from clients and customers in their assessments. Although having to manage four separate processes adds complexity, they all reinforce the new norm of continual feedback. And Weitzman-Garcia says the benefits to the organization far outweigh the costs to HR.

Coaching

The companies that most effectively adopt agile talent practices invest in sharpening managers' coaching skills. Supervisors at Cigna go through "coach" training designed for busy managers: It's broken into weekly 90-minute videos that can be viewed as people have time. The supervisors also engage in learning sessions, which, like "learning sprints" in agile project management, are brief and spread out to allow individuals to reflect and test-drive new skills on the job. Peer-to-peer feedback is incorporated in Cigna's manager training too: Colleagues form learning cohorts to share ideas and tactics. They're having the kinds of conversations companies want supervisors to have with their direct reports, but they feel freer to share mistakes with one another, without the fear of "evaluation" hanging over their heads.

DigitalOcean, a New York–based start-up focused on software as a service (SaaS) infrastructure, engages a full-time professional coach on-site to help all managers give better feedback to employees and, more broadly, to develop internal coaching capabilities. The idea is that once one experiences good coaching, one becomes a better coach. Not everyone is expected to become a great coach—those in the company who prefer coding to coaching can advance along a technical career track—but coaching skills are considered central to a managerial career.

P&G, too, is intent on making managers better coaches. That's part of a larger effort to rebuild training and development for supervisors and enhance their role in the organization. By simplifying the performance review process, separating evaluation from development discussions, and eliminating talent calibration sessions (the arbitrary horse trading between supervisors that often comes with a subjective and politicized ranking model), P&G has freed up a lot of time to devote to employees' growth. But getting supervisors to move from judging employees to coaching them in their day-to-day work has been a challenge in P&G's tradition-rich culture. So the company has invested heavily in training supervisors on topics such as how to establish employees' priorities and goals, how to provide feedback about contributions, and how to align employees' career aspirations with business needs and learning and development plans. The bet is that building employees' capabilities and relationships with supervisors will increase engagement and therefore help the company innovate and move faster. Even though the jury is still out on the company-wide culture shift, P&G is already reporting improvements in these areas, at all levels of management.

Teams

Traditional HR focused on individuals—their goals, their performance, their needs. But now that so many companies are organizing their work project by project, their management and talent systems are becoming more team focused. Groups are creating, executing, and revising their goals and tasks with scrums—at the team level, in the moment, to adapt quickly to new information as it comes in. ("Scrum" may be the best-known term in the agile lexicon. It comes from rugby, where players pack tightly together to restart play.) They are also taking it upon themselves to track their own progress, identify obstacles, assess their leadership, and generate insights about how to improve performance.

In that context, organizations must learn to contend with:

Multidirectional feedback. Peer feedback is essential to course corrections and employee development in an agile environment, because team members know better than anyone else what each person is contributing. It's rarely a formal process, and comments are generally directed to the employee, not the supervisor. That keeps input constructive and prevents the undermining of colleagues that sometimes occurs in hypercompetitive workplaces.

But some executives believe that peer feedback should have an impact on performance evaluations. Diane Gherson, IBM's head of HR, explains that "the relationships between managers and employees change in the context of a network [the collection of projects across which employees work]." Because an agile environment makes it practically impossible to "monitor" performance in the old sense, managers at IBM solicit input from others to help them identify and address issues early on. Unless it's sensitive, that input is shared in the team's daily stand-up meetings and captured in an app. Employees may choose whether to include managers and others in their comments to peers. The risk of cutthroat behavior is mitigated by the fact that peer comments to the supervisor also go to the team. Anyone trying to undercut colleagues will be exposed.

In agile organizations, "upward" feedback from employees to team leaders and supervisors is highly valued too. The Mitre Corporation's not-for-profit research centers have taken steps to encourage it, but they're finding that this requires concentrated effort. They started with periodic confidential employee surveys and focus groups to discover which issues people wanted to discuss with their managers. HR then distilled that data for supervisors to inform their conversations with direct reports. However, employees were initially hesitant to provide upward feedback—even though it was anonymous and was used for development purposes only— because they weren't accustomed to voicing their thoughts about what management was doing.

Mitre also learned that the most critical factor in getting subordinates to be candid was having managers explicitly say that they wanted and appreciated comments. Otherwise people might worry, reasonably, that their leaders weren't really open to feedback and ready to apply it. As with any employee survey, soliciting upward feedback and not acting on it has a diminishing effect on participation; it erodes the hard-earned trust between employees and their managers. When Mitre's new performance-management and feedback process began, the CEO acknowledged that the research centers would need to iterate and make improvements. A revised system for upward feedback will roll out this year.

Because feedback flows in all directions on teams, many companies use technology to manage the sheer volume of it. Apps allow supervisors, coworkers, and clients to give one another immediate feedback from wherever they are. Crucially, supervisors can download all the comments later on, when it's time to do evaluations. In some apps, employees and supervisors can score progress on goals; at least one helps managers analyze conversations on project management platforms like Slack to provide feedback on collaboration. Cisco uses proprietary technology to collect weekly raw data, or "bread crumbs," from employees about their peers' performance. Such tools enable managers to see fluctuations in individual performance over time, even within teams. The apps don't provide an official record of performance, of course, and employees may want to discuss problems face-to-face to avoid having them recorded in a file that can be downloaded. We know that companies recognize and reward improvement as well as actual performance, however, so hiding problems may not always pay off for employees.

Frontline decision rights. The fundamental shift toward teams has also affected decision rights: Organizations are pushing them down to the front lines, equipping and empowering employees to operate more independently. But that's a huge behavioral change, and people need support to pull it off. Let's return to the Bank of Montreal example to illustrate how it can work. When BMO introduced agile teams to design some new customer services, senior leaders weren't quite ready to give up control, and the people under them were not used to taking it. So the bank embedded agile coaches in business teams. They began by putting everyone, including high-level executives, through "retrospectives"—regular reflection and feedback sessions held after each iteration. These are the agile version of after-action reviews; their purpose is to keep improving processes. Because the retrospectives quickly identified concrete successes, failures, and root causes, senior leaders at

BMO immediately recognized their value, which helped them get on board with agile generally and loosen their grip on decision making.

Complex team dynamics. Finally, since the supervisor's role has moved away from just managing individuals and toward the much more complicated task of promoting productive, healthy team dynamics, people often need help with that, too. Cisco's special Team Intelligence unit provides that kind of support. It's charged with identifying the company's best-performing teams, analyzing how they operate, and helping other teams learn how to become more like them. It uses an enterprisewide platform called Team Space, which tracks data on team projects, needs, and achievements to both measure and improve what teams are doing within units and across the company.

Compensation

Pay is changing as well. A simple adaptation to agile work, seen in retail companies such as Macy's, is to use spot bonuses to recognize contributions when they happen rather than rely solely on end-of-year salary increases. Research and practice have shown that compensation works best as a motivator when it comes as soon as possible after the desired behavior. Instant rewards reinforce instant feedback in a powerful way. Annual merit-based raises are less effective, because too much time goes by.

Patagonia has actually eliminated annual raises for its knowledge workers. Instead the company adjusts wages for each job much more frequently, according to research on where market rates are going. Increases can also be allocated when employees take on more-difficult projects or go above and beyond in other ways. The company retains a budget for the top 1% of individual contributors, and supervisors can make a case for any contribution that merits that designation, including contributions to teams.

Compensation is also being used to reinforce agile values such as learning and knowledge sharing. In the start-up world, for instance, the online clothing-rental company Rent the Runway dropped separate bonuses, rolling the money into base pay. CEO Jennifer Hyman reports that the bonus program was getting in the way of honest peer feedback. Employees weren't sharing constructive criticism, knowing it could have negative financial consequences for their colleagues. The new system prevents that problem by "untangling the two," Hyman says.

DigitalOcean redesigned its rewards to promote equitable treatment of employees and a culture of collaboration. Salary adjustments now happen twice a year to respond to changes in the outside labor market and in jobs and performance. More important, DigitalOcean has closed gaps in pay for equivalent work. It's deliberately heading off internal rivalry, painfully aware of the problems in hypercompetitive cultures (think Microsoft and Amazon). To personalize compensation, the firm maps where people are having impact in their roles and where they need to grow and develop. The data on individuals' impact on the business is a key factor in discussions about pay. Negotiating to raise your own salary is fiercely discouraged. And only the top 1% of achievement is rewarded financially; otherwise, there is no merit-pay process. All employees are eligible for bonuses, which are based on company performance rather than individual contributions. To further support collaboration, DigitalOcean is diversifying its portfolio of rewards to include nonfinancial, meaningful gifts, such as a Kindle loaded with the CEO's "best books" picks.

How does DigitalOcean motivate people to perform their best without inflated financial rewards? Matt Hoffman, its vice president of people, says it focuses on creating a culture that inspires purpose and creativity. So far that seems to be working. The latest engagement survey, via Culture Amp, ranks DigitalOcean 17 points above the industry benchmark in satisfaction with compensation.

Recruiting

With the improvements in the economy since the Great Recession, recruiting and hiring have become more urgent—and more agile. To scale up quickly in 2015, GE's new digital division pioneered some interesting recruiting experiments. For instance, a cross-functional team works together on all hiring requisitions. A "head count manager" represents the interests of internal stakeholders who want their positions filled quickly and appropriately. Hiring managers rotate on and off the team, depending on whether they're currently hiring, and a scrum master oversees the process.

To keep things moving, the team focuses on vacancies that have cleared all the hurdles—no req's get started if debate is still ongoing about the desired attributes of candidates. Openings are ranked, and the team concentrates on the top-priority hires until they are completed. It works on several hires at once so that members can share information about candidates who may fit better in other roles. The team keeps track of its cycle time for filling positions and monitors all open requisitions on a kanban board to identify bottlenecks and blocked processes. IBM now takes a similar approach to recruitment.

Companies are also relying more heavily on technology to find and track candidates who are well suited to an agile work environment. GE, IBM, and Cisco are working with the vendor Ascendify to create software that does just this. The IT recruiting company HackerRank offers an online tool for the same purpose.

Learning and development

Like hiring, L&D had to change to bring new skills into organizations more quickly. Most companies already have a suite of online learning modules that employees can access on demand. Although helpful for those who have clearly defined needs, this is a bit like giving a student the key to a library and telling her to figure out what she must know and then learn it. Newer approaches use data analysis to identify the skills required for particular jobs and for advancement and then suggest to individual employees what kinds of training and future jobs make sense for them, given their experience and interests.

IBM uses artificial intelligence to generate such advice, starting with employees' profiles, which include prior and current roles, expected career trajectory, and training programs completed. The company has also created special training for agile environments—using, for example, animated simulations built around a series of "personas" to illustrate useful behaviors, such as offering constructive criticism.

What HR Can Learn from Tech

THE AGILE PIONEERS in the tech world are years ahead of everyone else in adopting the methodology at scale. So who better to provide guidance as managers and HR leaders grapple with how to apply agile talent practices throughout their organizations? In a recent survey, thousands of software developers across many countries and industries identified their biggest obstacles in scaling and the ways they got past them.

Top challenges with scaling...

Company culture at odds with agile value	63%
Lack of experience with methods	47
Lack of management support	45
Organizational resistance to change	43
Lack of business/culture/product owner	41
Insufficient training	34
Pervasiveness of traditional development	34
Inconsistent agile practices/process	31
Fragmented tooling, data, and measurements	20
Ineffective collaboration	19
Regulatory compliance and governance	15

... and elements needed for success

Internal agile coaches	52%
Executive sponsorship	48
Consistent process and practices	41
Implementation of a common tool across teams	36
Agile consultants or trainers	36

Source: VersionOne's 2016 State of Agile survey
Note: Respondents could make multiple selections.

Traditionally, L&D has included succession planning—the epitome of top-down, long-range thinking, whereby individuals are picked years in advance to take on the most crucial leadership roles, usually in the hope that they will develop certain capabilities on schedule. The world often fails to cooperate with those plans, though. Companies routinely find that by the time senior leadership positions open up, their needs have changed. The most common solution is to ignore the plan and start a search from scratch. But organizations often continue doing long-term succession planning anyway. (About half of large companies have a plan to develop successors for the top job.) Pepsi is one company taking a simple step away from this model by shortening the time frame. It provides brief quarterly updates on the development of possible successors—in contrast to the usual annual updates—and delays appointments so that they happen closer to when successors are likely to step into their roles.

Ongoing Challenges

To be sure, not every organization or group is in hot pursuit of rapid innovation. Some jobs must remain largely rules based. (Consider the work that accountants, nuclear control-room operators, and surgeons do.) In such cases agile talent practices may not make sense.

And even when they're appropriate, they may meet resistance—especially within HR. A lot of processes have to change for an organization to move away from a planning-based "waterfall" model (which is linear rather than flexible and adaptive), and some of them are hardwired into information systems, job titles, and so forth. The move toward cloud-based IT, which is happening independently, has made it easier to adopt app-based tools. But people issues remain a sticking point. Many HR tasks, such as traditional approaches to recruitment, onboarding, and program coordination, will become obsolete, as will expertise in those areas.

Meanwhile, new tasks are being created. Helping supervisors replace judging with coaching is a big challenge not just in terms of skills but also because it undercuts their status and formal authority. Shifting the focus of management from individuals to teams may be even more difficult, because team dynamics can be a black box to those who are still struggling to understand how to coach individuals. The big question is whether companies can help managers take all this on and see the value in it.

The HR function will also require reskilling. It will need more expertise in IT support—especially given all the performance data generated by the new apps—and deeper knowledge about teams and hands-on supervision. HR has not had to change in recent decades nearly as much as have the line operations it supports. But now the pressure is on, and it's coming from the operating level, which makes it much harder to cling to old talent practices.

Originally published in March–April 2018. Reprint R1802B

Reinventing Performance Management

by Marcus Buckingham and Ashley Goodall

AT DELOITTE WE'RE REDESIGNING our performance management system. This may not surprise you. Like many other companies, we realize that our current process for evaluating the work of our people—and then training them, promoting them, and paying them accordingly—is increasingly out of step with our objectives. In a public survey Deloitte conducted recently, more than half the executives questioned (58%) believe that their current performance management approach drives neither employee engagement nor high performance. They, and we, are in need of something nimbler, real-time, and more individualized—something squarely focused on fueling performance in the future rather than assessing it in the past.

What might surprise you, however, is what we'll include in Deloitte's new system and what we won't. It will have no cascading objectives, no once-a-year reviews, and no 360-degree-feedback tools. We've arrived at a very different and much simpler design for managing people's performance. Its hallmarks are speed, agility, one-size-fits-one, and constant learning, and it's underpinned by a new way of collecting reliable performance data. This system will make much more sense for our talent-dependent business. But we might never have arrived at its design without drawing on three pieces of evidence: a simple counting of hours, a review of research in the science of ratings, and a carefully controlled study of our own organization.

Counting and the Case for Change

More than likely, the performance management system Deloitte has been using has some characteristics in common with yours. Objectives are set for each of our 65,000-plus people at the beginning of the year; after a project is finished, each person's manager rates him or her on how well those objectives were met. The manager also comments on where the person did or didn't excel. These evaluations are factored into a single year-end rating, arrived at in lengthy "consensus meetings" at which groups of "counselors" discuss hundreds of people in light of their peers.

Internal feedback demonstrates that our people like the predictability of this process and the fact that because each person is assigned a counselor, he or she has a representative at the consensus meetings. The vast majority of our people believe the process is fair. We realize, however, that it's no longer the best design for Deloitte's emerging needs: Once-a-year goals are too "batched" for a real-time world, and conversations about year-end ratings are generally less valuable than conversations conducted in the moment about actual performance.

But the need for change didn't crystallize until we decided to count things. Specifically, we tallied the number of hours the organization was spending on performance management—and found that completing the forms, holding the meetings, and creating the ratings consumed close to *2 million hours a year*. As we studied how those hours were spent, we realized that many of them were eaten up by leaders' discussions behind closed doors about the outcomes of the process. We wondered if we could somehow shift our investment of time from talking to ourselves about ratings to talking to our people about their performance and careers—from a focus on the past to a focus on the future.

The Science of Ratings

Our next discovery was that assessing someone's *skills* produces inconsistent data. Objective as I may try to be in evaluating you on, say, strategic thinking, it turns out that how much strategic thinking *I* do, or how valuable *I* think strategic thinking is, or how tough

Idea in Brief

The Problem

Not just employees but their managers and even HR departments are by now questioning the conventional wisdom of performance management, including its common reliance on cascading objectives, backward-looking assessments, once-a-year rankings and reviews, and 360-degree-feedback tools.

The Goal

Some companies have ditched the rankings and even annual reviews, but they haven't found better solutions. Deloitte resolved to design a system that would fairly recognize varying performance, have a clear view into performance anytime, and boost performance in the future.

The Solution

Deloitte's new approach separates compensation decisions from day-to-day performance management, produces better insight through quarterly or per-project "performance snapshots," and relies on weekly check-ins with managers to keep performance on course.

a rater *I* am significantly affects my assessment of *your* strategic thinking.

How significantly? The most comprehensive research on what ratings actually measure was conducted by Michael Mount, Steven Scullen, and Maynard Goff and published in the *Journal of Applied Psychology* in 2000. Their study—in which 4,492 managers were rated on certain performance dimensions by two bosses, two peers, and two subordinates—revealed that 62% of the variance in the ratings could be accounted for by individual raters' peculiarities of perception. Actual performance accounted for only 21% of the variance. This led the researchers to conclude (in *How People Evaluate Others in Organizations,* edited by Manuel London): "Although it is implicitly assumed that the ratings measure the performance of the ratee, most of what is being measured by the ratings is the unique rating tendencies of the rater. Thus ratings reveal more about the rater than they do about the ratee." This gave us pause. We wanted to understand performance at the individual level, and we knew that the person in the best position to judge it was the immediate team leader. But how could we capture a team leader's view of performance without running afoul of what the researchers termed "idiosyncratic rater effects"?

Putting Ourselves Under the Microscope

We also learned that the defining characteristic of the very best teams at Deloitte is that they are strengths oriented. Their members feel that they are called upon to do their best work every day. This discovery was not based on intuitive judgment or gleaned from anecdotes and hearsay; rather, it was derived from an empirical study of our own high-performing teams.

Our study built on previous research. Starting in the late 1990s, Gallup performed a multiyear examination of high-performing teams that eventually involved more than 1.4 million employees, 50,000 teams, and 192 organizations. Gallup asked both high- and lower-performing teams questions on numerous subjects, from mission and purpose to pay and career opportunities, and isolated the questions on which the high-performing teams strongly agreed and the rest did not. It found at the beginning of the study that almost all the variation between high- and lower-performing teams was explained by a very small group of items. The most powerful one proved to be "At work, I have the opportunity to do what I do best every day." Business units whose employees chose "strongly agree" for this item were 44% more likely to earn high customer satisfaction scores, 50% more likely to have low employee turnover, and 38% more likely to be productive.

We set out to see whether those results held at Deloitte. First we identified 60 high-performing teams, which involved 1,287 employees and represented all parts of the organization. For the control group, we chose a representative sample of 1,954 employees. To measure the conditions within a team, we employed a six-item survey. When the results were in and tallied, three items correlated best with high performance for a team: "My coworkers are committed to doing quality work," "The mission of our company inspires me," and "I have the chance to use my strengths every day." Of these, the third was the most powerful across the organization.

All this evidence helped bring into focus the problem we were trying to solve with our new design. We wanted to spend more time helping our people use their strengths—in teams characterized by great clarity of purpose and expectations—and we wanted a quick way to collect reliable and differentiated performance data. With this in mind, we set to work.

Radical Redesign

We began by stating as clearly as we could what performance management is actually *for,* at least as far as Deloitte is concerned. We articulated three objectives for our new system. The first was clear: It would allow us to *recognize* performance, particularly through variable compensation. Most current systems do this.

But to recognize each person's performance, we had to be able to *see* it clearly. That became our second objective. Here we faced two issues—the idiosyncratic rater effect and the need to streamline our traditional process of evaluation, project rating, consensus meeting, and final rating. The solution to the former requires a subtle shift in our approach. Rather than asking more people for their opinion of a team member (in a 360-degree or an upward-feedback survey, for example), we found that we will need to ask only the immediate team leader—but, critically, to ask a different kind of question. People may rate other people's skills inconsistently, but they are highly consistent when rating their own feelings and intentions. To see performance at the individual level, then, we will ask team leaders not about the *skills* of each team member but about their *own future actions* with respect to that person.

At the end of every project (or once every quarter for long-term projects) we will ask team leaders to respond to four future-focused statements about each team member. We've refined the wording of these statements through successive tests, and we know that at Deloitte they clearly highlight differences among individuals and reliably measure performance. Here are the four:

1. Given what I know of this person's performance, and if it were my money, I would award this person the highest possible compensation increase and bonus [*measures overall performance and unique value to the organization on a five-point scale from "strongly agree" to "strongly disagree"*].

2. Given what I know of this person's performance, I would always want him or her on my team [*measures ability to work well with others on the same five-point scale*].

3. This person is at risk for low performance [*identifies problems that might harm the customer or the team on a yes-or-no basis*].

4. This person is ready for promotion today [*measures potential on a yes-or-no basis*].

In effect, we are asking our team leaders what they would *do* with each team member rather than what they *think* of that individual. When we aggregate these data points over a year, weighting each according to the duration of a given project, we produce a rich stream of information for leaders' discussions of what they, in turn, will do—whether it's a question of succession planning, development paths, or performance-pattern analysis. Once a quarter the organization's leaders can use the new data to review a targeted subset of employees (those eligible for promotion, for example, or those with critical skills) and can debate what actions Deloitte might take to better develop that particular group. In this aggregation of simple but powerful data points, we see the possibility of shifting our 2-million-hour annual investment from talking about the ratings to talking about our people—from ascertaining the facts of performance to considering what we should do in response to those facts.

In addition to this consistent—and countable—data, when it comes to compensation, we want to factor in some uncountable things, such as the difficulty of project assignments in a given year and contributions to the organization other than formal projects. So the data will serve as the starting point for compensation, not the ending point. The final determination will be reached either by a leader who knows each individual personally or by a group of leaders looking at an entire segment of our practice and at many data points in parallel.

We could call this new evaluation a rating, but it bears no resemblance, in generation or in use, to the ratings of the past. Because it allows us to quickly capture performance at a single moment in time, we call it a *performance snapshot.*

The Third Objective

Two objectives for our new system, then, were clear: We wanted to recognize performance, and we had to be able to see it clearly. But all our research, all our conversations with leaders on the topic of performance management, and all the feedback from our people left us convinced that something was missing. Is performance management at root more about "management" or about "performance"? Put differently, although it may be great to be able to measure and reward the performance you have, wouldn't it be better still to be able to improve it?

Our third objective therefore became to *fuel* performance. And if the performance snapshot was an organizational tool for measuring it, we needed a tool that team leaders could use to strengthen it.

Research into the practices of the best team leaders reveals that they conduct regular check-ins with each team member about near-term work. These brief conversations allow leaders to set expectations for the upcoming week, review priorities, comment on recent work, and provide course correction, coaching, or important new information. The conversations provide clarity regarding what is expected of each team member and why, what great work looks like, and how each can do his or her best work in the upcoming days—in other words, exactly the trinity of purpose, expectations, and strengths that characterizes our best teams.

Our design calls for every team leader to check in with each team member once a week. For us, these check-ins are not *in addition* to the work of a team leader; they *are* the work of a team leader. If a leader checks in less often than once a week, the team member's priorities may become vague and aspirational, and the leader can't be as helpful—and the conversation will shift from coaching for near-term work to giving feedback about past performance. In other words, the content of these conversations will be a direct outcome of their frequency: If you want people to talk about how to do their best work in the near future, they need to talk often. And so far we have found in our testing a direct and measurable correlation between the frequency of these conversations and the engagement of team

Performance intelligence

In an early proof of concept of the redesigned system, executives in one large practice area at Deloitte called up data from project managers to consider important talent-related decisions. In the charts below, each dot represents an individual; decision makers could click on a dot to see the person's name and details from his or her "performance snapshots."

What are team leaders telling us?

*First the group looked at the whole story. This view plotted all the members of the practice according to how much their various project managers agreed with two statements: "I would always want this person on my team" (**y axis**) and "I would give this person the highest possible compensation" (**x axis**). The axes are the same for the other three screens.*

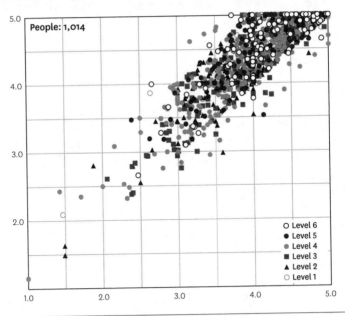

members. Very frequent check-ins (we might say *radically* frequent check-ins) are a team leader's killer app.

That said, team leaders have many demands on their time. We've learned that the best way to ensure frequency is to have check-ins be initiated by the team member—who more often than not is eager for

How would this data help determine pay?

Next the data was filtered to look only at individuals at a given job level. A fundamental question for performance management systems is whether they can capture enough variation among people to fairly allocate pay. A data distribution like this offers a starting point for broader discussion.

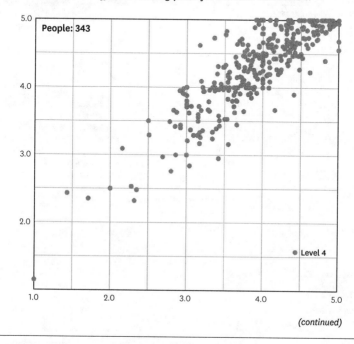

(continued)

the guidance and attention they provide—rather than by the team leader.

To support both people in these conversations, our system will allow individual members to understand and explore their strengths using a self-assessment tool and then to present those strengths to their teammates, their team leader, and the rest of the organization. Our reasoning is twofold. First, as we've seen, people's strengths generate their highest performance today and the greatest improvement in their performance tomorrow, and so deserve to be a central focus. Second, if we want to see frequent (weekly!) use of our system, we have to think of it as a consumer technology—that is, designed to be simple, quick, and above all engaging to use. Many of the successful

How would it help guide promotions?

This view was filtered to show individuals whose team leaders responded "yes" to the statement "This person is ready for promotion today." The data supports objectivity in annual executive discussions about advancement.

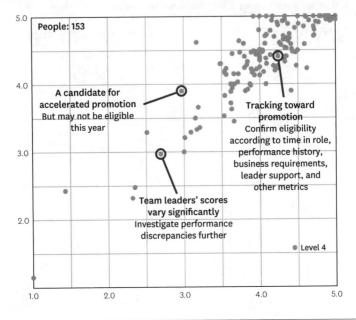

consumer technologies of the past several years (particularly social media) are *sharing* technologies, which suggests that most of us are consistently interested in ourselves—our own insights, achievements, and impact. So we want this new system to provide a place for people to explore and share what is best about themselves.

Transparency

This is where we are today: We've defined three objectives at the root of performance management—to *recognize, see,* and *fuel* performance. We have three interlocking rituals to support them—the annual compensation decision, the quarterly or per-project

How would it help address low performance?

This view was filtered to show individuals whose team leaders responded "yes" to the statement "This person is at risk of low performance." As the upper right of this screen shows, even high performers can slip up—and it's important that the organization help them recover.

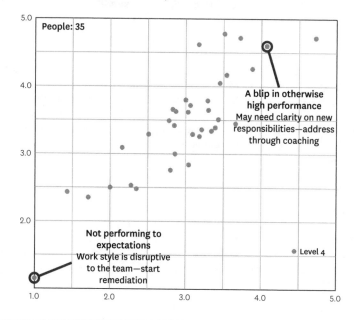

performance snapshot, and the weekly check-in. And we've shifted from a batched focus on the past to a continual focus on the future, through regular evaluations and frequent check-ins. As we've tested each element of this design with ever-larger groups across Deloitte, we've seen that the change can be an evolution over time: Different business units can introduce a strengths orientation first, then more-frequent conversations, then new ways of measuring, and finally new software for monitoring performance. (See the exhibit "Performance intelligence.")

But one issue has surfaced again and again during this work, and that's the issue of transparency. When an organization knows

How Deloitte Built a Radically Simple Performance Measure

ONE OF THE MOST IMPORTANT TOOLS in our redesigned performance management system is the "performance snapshot." It lets us see performance quickly and reliably across the organization, freeing us to spend more time engaging with our people. Here's how we created it.

1. The Criteria

We looked for measures that met three criteria. To neutralize the idiosyncratic rater effect, we wanted raters to rate their own actions, rather than the qualities or behaviors of the ratee. To generate the necessary range, the questions had to be phrased in the extreme. And to avoid confusion, each one had to contain a single, easily understood concept. We chose one about pay, one about teamwork, one about poor performance, and one about promotion. Those categories may or may not be right for other organizations, but they work for us.

2. The Rater

We were looking for someone with vivid experience of the individual's performance and whose subjective judgment we felt was important. We agreed that team leaders are closest to the performance of ratees and, by virtue of their roles, must exercise subjective judgment. We could have included functional managers, or even ratees' peers, but we wanted to start with clarity and simplicity.

3. Testing

We then tested that our questions would produce useful data. Validity testing focuses on their difficulty (as revealed by mean responses) and the

---

something about us, and that knowledge is captured in a number, we often feel entitled to know it—to know where we stand. We suspect that this issue will need its own radical answer.

In the first version of our design, we kept the results of performance snapshots from the team member. We did this because we knew from the past that when an evaluation is to be shared, the responses skew high—that is, they are sugarcoated. Because we range of responses (as revealed by standard deviations). We knew that if they consistently yielded a tight cluster of "strongly agree" responses, we wouldn't get the differentiation we were looking for. *Construct* validity and *criterion-related* validity are also important. (That is, the questions should collectively test an underlying theory and make it possible to find correlations with outcomes measured in other ways, such as engagement surveys.)

4. Frequency

At Deloitte we live and work in a project structure, so it makes sense for us to produce a performance snapshot at the end of each project. For longer-term projects we've decided that quarterly is the best frequency. Our goal is to strike the right balance between tying the evaluation as tightly as possible to the experience of the performance and not overburdening our team leaders, lest survey fatigue yield poor data.

5. Transparency

We're experimenting with this now. We want our snapshots to reveal the real-time "truth" of what our team leaders think, yet our experience tells us that if they know that team members will see every data point, they may be tempted to sugarcoat the results to avoid difficult conversations. We know that we'll aggregate an individual's snapshot scores into an annual composite. But what, exactly, should we share at year's end? We want to err on the side of sharing more, not less—to aggregate snapshot scores not only for client work but also for internal projects, along with performance metrics such as hours and sales, in the context of a group of peers—so that we can give our people the richest possible view of where they stand. Time will tell how close to that ideal we can get.

wanted to capture unfiltered assessments, we made the responses private. We worried that otherwise we might end up destroying the very truth we sought to reveal.

But what, in fact, is that truth? What do we see when we try to quantify a person? In the world of sports, we have pages of statistics for each player; in medicine, a three-page report each time we get blood work done; in psychometric evaluations, a battery of tests and percentiles. At work, however, at least when it comes to quantifying performance, we try to express the infinite variety and nuance of a human being in a single number.

Surely, however, a better understanding comes from conversations—with your team leader about how you're doing, or between leaders as they consider your compensation or your career. And these conversations are best served not by a single data point but by many. If we want to do our best to tell you where you stand, we must capture as much of your diversity as we can and then talk about it.

We haven't resolved this issue yet, but here's what we're asking ourselves and testing: What's the most detailed view of you that we can gather and share? How does that data support a conversation about your performance? How can we equip our leaders to have insightful conversations? Our question now is not *What is the simplest view of you?* but *What is the richest?*

Over the past few years the debate about performance management has been characterized as a debate about ratings—whether or not they are fair, and whether or not they achieve their stated objectives. But perhaps the issue is different: not so much that ratings fail to convey what the organization knows about each person but that as presented, that knowledge is sadly one-dimensional. In the end, it's not the particular number we assign to a person that's the problem; rather, it's the fact that there *is* a single number. Ratings are a distillation of the truth—and up until now, one might argue, a necessary one. Yet we want our organizations to know us, and we want to know ourselves at work, and that can't be compressed into a single number. We now have the technology to go from a small data version of our people to a big data version of them. As we scale up our new approach across Deloitte, that's the issue we want to solve next.

Originally published in April 2015. Reprint R1504B

Better People Analytics

by Paul Leonardi and Noshir Contractor

"WE HAVE CHARTS AND GRAPHS to back us up. So f*** off." New hires in Google's people analytics department began receiving a laptop sticker with that slogan a few years ago, when the group probably felt it needed to defend its work. Back then people analytics—using statistical insights from employee data to make talent management decisions—was still a provocative idea with plenty of skeptics who feared it might lead companies to reduce individuals to numbers. HR collected data on workers, but the notion that it could be actively mined to understand and manage them was novel—and suspect.

Today there's no need for stickers. More than 70% of companies now say they consider people analytics to be a high priority. The field even has celebrated case studies, like Google's Project Oxygen, which uncovered the practices of the tech giant's best managers and then used them in coaching sessions to improve the work of low performers. Other examples, such as Dell's experiments with increasing the success of its sales force, also point to the power of people analytics.

But hype, as it often does, has outpaced reality. The truth is, people analytics has made only modest progress over the past decade. A survey by Tata Consultancy Services found that just 5% of big-data investments go to HR, the group that typically manages people analytics. And a recent study by Deloitte showed that although people analytics has become mainstream, only 9% of companies believe they have a good understanding of which talent dimensions drive performance in their organizations.

What gives? If, as the sticker says, people analytics teams have charts and graphs to back them up, why haven't results followed? We believe it's because most rely on a narrow approach to data analysis: They use data only about individual people, when data about the interplay *among* people is equally or more important.

People's interactions are the focus of an emerging discipline we call *relational analytics.* By incorporating it into their people analytics strategies, companies can better identify employees who are capable of helping them achieve their goals, whether for increased innovation, influence, or efficiency. Firms will also gain insight into which key players they can't afford to lose and where silos exist in their organizations.

Fortunately, the raw material for relational analytics already exists in companies. It's the data created by e-mail exchanges, chats, and file transfers—the *digital exhaust* of a company. By mining it, firms can build good relational analytics models.

In this article we present a framework for understanding and applying relational analytics. And we have the charts and graphs to back us up.

Relational Analytics: A Deeper Definition

To date, people analytics has focused mostly on employee *attribute* data, of which there are two kinds:

- *Trait:* facts about individuals that don't change, such as ethnicity, gender, and work history

- *State:* facts about individuals that do change, such as age, education level, company tenure, value of received bonuses, commute distance, and days absent

The two types of data are often aggregated to identify group characteristics, such as ethnic makeup, gender diversity, and average compensation.

Attribute analytics is necessary but not sufficient. Aggregate attribute data may seem like relational data because it involves

Idea in Brief

The Challenge

To bring the performance of people analytics up—and in line with the hype—companies need to do more than analyze data on demographic attributes.

The Solution

Employ relational analytics, which examines data on how people interact, to find out who has good ideas, who is influential, what teams will get work done on time, and more.

The Raw Material

Companies can mine their "digital exhaust"—data created by employees every day in their digital transactions, such as e-mails, chats, and file collaboration—for insights into their workforce.

more than one person, but it's not. Relational data captures, for example, the communications between two people in different departments in a day. In short, relational analytics is the science of human social networks.

Decades of research convincingly show that the relationships employees have with one another—together with their individual attributes—can explain their workplace performance. The key is finding "structural signatures": patterns in the data that correlate to some form of good (or bad) performance. Just as neurologists can identify structural signatures in the brain's networks that predict bipolar disorder and schizophrenia, and chemists can look at the structural signatures of a liquid and predict its kinetic fragility, organizational leaders can look at structural signatures in their companies' social networks and predict how, say, creative or effective individual employees, teams, or the organization as a whole will be.

The Six Signatures of Relational Analytics

Drawing from our own research and our consulting work with companies, as well as from a large body of other scholars' research, we have identified six structural signatures that should form the bedrock of any relational analytics strategy.

Let's look at each one in turn.

Ideation

Most companies try to identify people who are good at ideation by examining attributes like educational background, experience, personality, and native intelligence. Those things are important, but they don't help us see people's access to information from others or the diversity of their sources of information—both of which are arguably even more important. Good idea generators often synthesize information from one team with information from another to develop a new product concept. Or they use a solution created in one division to solve a problem in another. In other words, they occupy a brokerage position in networks.

The sociologist Ronald Burt has developed a measure that indicates whether someone is in a brokerage position. Known as *constraint,* it captures how limited a person is when gathering unique information. Study after study, across populations as diverse as bankers, lawyers, analysts, engineers, and software developers, has shown that employees with low constraint—who aren't bound by a small, tight network of people—are more likely to generate ideas that management views as novel and useful.

In one study, Burt followed the senior leaders at a large U.S. electronics company as they applied relational analytics to determine which of 600-plus supply chain managers were most likely to develop ideas that improved efficiency. They used a survey to solicit such ideas from the managers and at the same time gather information on their networks. Senior executives then scored each of the submitted ideas for their novelty and potential value.

The only attribute that remotely predicted whether an individual would generate a valuable idea was seniority at the company, and its correlation wasn't strong. Using the ideation signature—low constraint—was far more powerful: Supply chain managers who exhibited it in their networks were significantly more likely to generate good ideas than managers with high constraint.

A study Paul did at a large software development company bolsters this finding. The company's R&D department was a

Ideation signature

*Black shows **low constraint**: He communicates with people in several other networks besides his own, which makes him more likely to get novel information that will lead to good ideas. Dark gray, who communicates only with people within his network, is less likely to generate ideas, even though he may be creative.*

Focus: Individual
Predicts: Which employees will come up with good ideas

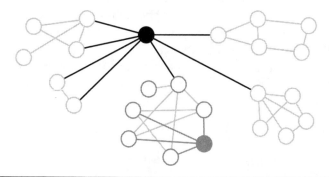

"caveman world." Though it employed more than 100 engineers, on average each one talked to only five other people. And those five people typically talked only to one another. Their contact with other "caves" was limited.

Such high-constraint networks are quite common in organizations, especially those that do specialized work. But that doesn't mean low-constraint individuals aren't hiding in plain sight. At the software company, relational analytics was able to pinpoint a few engineers who did span multiple networks. Management then generated a plan for encouraging them to do what they were naturally inclined to and soon saw a significant increase in both the quantity—and quality—of ideas they proposed for product improvements.

Influence

Developing a good idea is no guarantee that people will use it. Similarly, just because an executive issues a decree for change, that doesn't mean employees will carry it out. Getting ideas implemented requires influence.

But influence doesn't work the way we might assume. Research shows that employees are not most influenced, positively or negatively, by the company's senior leadership. Rather, it's people in less formal roles who sway them the most.

If that's the case, executives should just identify the popular employees and have them persuade their coworkers to get on board with new initiatives, right? Wrong.

A large medical device manufacturer that Paul worked with tried that approach when it was launching new compliance policies. Hoping to spread positive perceptions about them, the change

---

Influence signature

*Though she connects to only two people, black is more influential than dark gray, because black's connections are better connected. Black shows **higher aggregate prominence**. Dark gray may spread ideas faster, but black can spread ideas further because her connections are more influential.*

Focus: Individual
Predicts: Which employees will change others' behavior

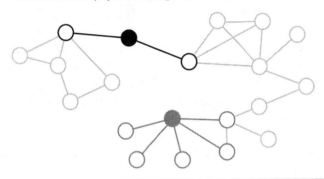

---

management team shared the policies' virtues with the workers who had been rated influential by the highest number of colleagues. But six months later employees still weren't following the new procedures.

Why? A counterintuitive insight from relational analytics offers the explanation: Employees cited as influential by a large number of colleagues aren't always the most influential people. Rather, the greatest influencers are people who have strong connections to others, even if only to a few people. Moreover, their strong connections in turn have strong connections of their own with other people. This means influencers' ideas can spread further.

The structural signature of influence is called *aggregate prominence,* and it's computed by measuring how well a person's connections are connected, and how well the connections' connections are connected. (A similar logic is used by search engines to rank-order search results.)

In each of nine divisions at the medical device manufacturer, relational analytics identified the five individuals who had the highest aggregate prominence scores. The company asked for their thoughts on the new policies. About three-quarters viewed them favorably. The firm provided facts that would allay fears of the change to them as well as to the influencers who didn't like the policies—and then waited for the results.

Six months later more than 75% of the employees in those nine divisions had adopted the new compliance policies. In contrast, only 15% of employees had adopted them in the remaining seven affected divisions, where relational analytics had not been applied.

Efficiency

Staffing a team that will get work done efficiently seems as if it should be simple. Just tap the people who have the best relevant skills.

Attribute analytics can help identify skilled people, but it won't ensure that the work gets done on time. For that, you need relational analytics measuring team chemistry and the ability to draw on outside information and expertise.

Consider the findings of a study by Ray Reagans, Ezra Zuckerman, and Bill McEvily, which analyzed more than 1,500 project teams at a major U.S. contract R&D firm. Hypothesizing that the ability to access a wide range of information, perspectives, and resources would improve team performance, the researchers compared the effect of demographic diversity on teams' results with the effect of team members' social networks. One issue was that diversity at the firm had only two real variables, tenure and function. (The other variables—race, gender, and education—were consolidated within functions.) Nevertheless, the results showed that diversity in those two areas had little impact on performance.

Turning to the relational data, though, offered better insight. The researchers found that two social variables were associated

---

Efficiency signature

The black team members are deeply connected with one another—showing **high internal density**. *This indicates that they work well together. And because members' external connections don't overlap, the team has* **high external range**, *which gives it greater access to helpful outside resources.*

Focus: Team
Predicts: Which teams will complete projects on time

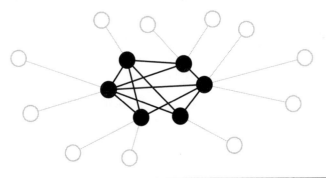

---

with higher performance. The first was *internal density,* the amount of interaction and interconnectedness among team members. High internal density is critical for building trust, taking risks, and reaching agreement on important issues. The second was the *external range* of team members' contacts. On a team that has high external range, each member can reach outside the team to experts who are distinct from the contacts of other members. That makes the team better able to source vital information and secure resources it needs to meet deadlines. The structural signature for efficient teams is therefore high internal density plus high external range.

At the R&D firm the teams that had this signature completed projects much faster than teams that did not. The researchers estimated that if 30% of project teams at the firm had internal density and external range just one standard deviation above the mean, it would save more than 2,200 labor hours in 17 days—the equivalent of completing nearly 200 additional projects.

Innovation

Teams with the efficiency signature would most likely fail as innovation units, which benefit from some disagreement and strife.

What else makes for a successful team of innovators? You might think that putting your highest-performing employees together would produce the best results, but research suggests that it might have negative effects on performance. And while the conventional wisdom is that teams are more creative when they comprise members with different points of view, research also indicates that demographic diversity is not a good predictor of team innovation success. In our experience, even staffing an innovation team with ideators often produces no better than average performance.

But if you turn to relational analytics, you can use the same variables you use for team efficiency—internal density and external range—to create promising innovation teams. The formula is a bit different, though: The innovation signature is high external range and low internal density. That is, you still want team members with wide, nonoverlapping social networks (influential ones, if possible)

Innovation signature

*Black team members aren't deeply interconnected; their team has **low internal density**. This suggests they'll have different perspectives and more-productive debates. The members also have **high external range**, or wide, diverse connections, which will help them gain buy-in for their innovations.*

Focus: Team
Predicts: Which teams will innovate effectively

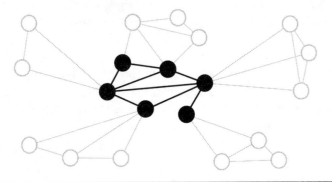

to source diverse ideas and information. But you do not want a tight-knit team.

Why? Greater interaction within a team results in similar ways of thinking and less discord. That's good for efficiency but not for innovation. The most innovative teams have disagreements and discussion—sometimes even conflict—that generate the creative friction necessary to produce breakthroughs.

The high external range is needed not just to bring in ideas but also to garner support and buy-in. Innovation teams have to finance, build, and sell their ideas, so well-connected external contacts who become the teams' champions can have a big impact on their success.

For several years, Paul worked with a large U.S.-based automobile company that was trying to improve its product-development process. Each of its global product-development centers had a team of subject-matter experts focused on that challenge. The program leader noted, "We are very careful about who we select. We get the people with the right functional backgrounds, who have consistently done innovative work, and we make sure there is a mix of them from different backgrounds and that they are different ages." In other words, the centers used attribute analytics to form teams.

Managers at a new India center couldn't build a demographically diverse team, however: All the center's engineers were roughly the same age, had similar backgrounds, and were about the same rank. So the manager instead chose engineers who had worked on projects with different offices and worked in different areas of the center—creating a team that naturally had a higher external range.

It so happened that such a team showed lower internal density as well. Its members felt free to debate, and they ran tests to resolve differences of opinion. Once they found a new procedure, they went back to their external connections, using them as influencers who could persuade others to validate their work.

After three years the India center's team was producing more process innovations than any of the other teams. After five years it had generated almost twice as many as all the other teams combined. In response, the company began supplementing its attribute analytics with relational analytics to reconfigure the innovation teams at its other locations.

Silos

Everyone hates silos, but they're natural and unavoidable. As organizations develop deep areas of expertise, almost inevitably functions, departments, and divisions become less and less able to work together. They don't speak the same technical language or have the same goals.

We assess the degree to which an organization is siloed by measuring its *modularity*. Most simply, modularity is the ratio of communication within a group to communication outside the group. When the ratio of internal to external communication is greater than 5:1, the group is detrimentally siloed.

Silo signature

*Each grouping indicates a department. People within the departments are deeply connected, but only one or two people in any department connect with people in other departments. The groups' **modularity**—the ratio of internal to external communication—is high.*

Focus: Organization
Predicts: Whether an organization is siloed

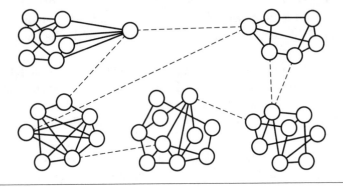

One of the most strikingly siloed organizations we've encountered was a small not-for-profit consumer advocacy group, which wanted to understand why traffic on its website had declined. The 60 employees at its Chicago office were divided among four departments: business development, operations, marketing and PR, and finance. Typical of silos, each department had different ideas about what was going on.

Analysis showed that all four departments exceeded the 5:1 ratio of internal to external contacts. The most extreme case was operations, with a ratio of 13:1. Of course, operations was the department with its finger most squarely on the pulse of consumers who visited the site. It sat on a trove of data about when and why people came to the site to complain about or praise companies.

Other departments didn't even know that operations collected that data. And operations didn't know that other departments might find it useful.

To fix the problem, the organization asked specific employees in each department to become liaisons. They instituted a weekly meeting at which managers from all departments got together to talk about their work. Each meeting was themed, so lower-level employees whose work related to the theme also were brought into the discussions.

In short, the not-for-profit engineered higher external range into its staff. As a result, operations learned that marketing and PR could make hay out of findings that linked a growing volume of complaints in a specific industry to certain weather patterns and seasons. Because operations employees learned that such insights would be useful, they began to analyze their data in new ways.

Vulnerability

Although having people who can help move information and insights from one part of the organization to another is healthy, an overreliance on those individuals can make a company vulnerable.

Take the case of an employee we'll call Arvind, who was a manager in the packaging division at one of the world's top consumer goods companies. He was a connector who bridged several divisions. He talked regularly with counterparts and suppliers across the world. But on the organizational chart, Arvind was nobody special: just a midlevel manager who was good at his job. Companies are at risk of losing employees like Arvind because no obvious attribute signals their importance, so firms don't know what they've got until it's gone.

Without Arvind, the packaging division would lack *robustness*. Networks are robust when connections can be maintained if you remove nodes—employees—from it. In this case, if Arvind left the company, some departments would lose all connection with other departments and with suppliers.

Vulnerability signature

Black is a critical external supplier to other company departments. Six people at the company have relationships with black, but 30 people rely on those relationships—which puts the company at risk. If dark gray's one connection to black leaves, for example, the department will be cut off from the supplier. While his title may not reflect his importance, that employee is vital to information flow.

Focus: Organization
Predicts: Which employees the organization can't afford to lose

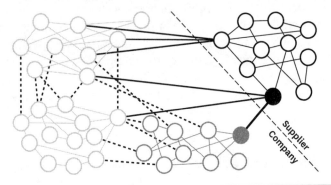

It wasn't that Arvind was irreplaceable. He just wasn't *backed up.* The company didn't realize that no other nodes were making the necessary network connections he provided. That made it vulnerable: If Arvind was out sick or on vacation, work slowed. If Arvind decided that he didn't like one of the suppliers and stopped interacting with it, work slowed. And if Arvind had too much on his plate and couldn't keep up with his many connections, work also slowed.

On the day Noshir came to show the company this vulnerability in the packaging division, he entered a boardroom filled with cakes and sweets. A senior executive happily told him that the firm was throwing a party for Arvind. He was retiring. Noshir's jaw dropped. The party went on, but after learning how important Arvind was, the company worked out a deal to retain him for several more years and, in the meantime, used relational analytics to do some succession planning so that multiple people could take on his role.

Capture Your Company's Digital Exhaust

Once you understand the six structural signatures that form the basis of relational analytics, it's relatively easy to act on the insights they provide. Often, the fixes they suggest aren't complex: Set up cross-functional meetings, enable influential people, retain your Arvinds.

Why, then, don't most companies use relational analytics for performance management? There are two reasons. The first is that many network analyses companies do are little more than pretty pictures of nodes and edges. They don't identify the patterns that predict performance.

The second reason is that most organizations don't have information systems in place to capture relational data. But all companies do have a crucial hidden resource: their digital exhaust—the logs, e-trails, and contents of everyday digital activity. Every time employees send one another e-mails in Outlook, message one another on Slack, like posts on Facebook's Workplace, form teams in Microsoft Teams, or assign people to project milestones in Trello, the platforms record the interactions. This information can be used to construct views of employee, team, and organizational networks in which you can pick out the structural signatures we've discussed.

For several years we've been developing a dashboard that captures digital exhaust in real time from these various platforms and uses relational analytics to help managers find the right employees for tasks, staff teams for efficiency and innovation, and identify areas in the organization that are siloed and vulnerable to turnover. Here are some of the things we've learned in the process:

Passive collection is easier on employees

To gather relational data, companies typically survey employees about whom they interact with. Surveys take time, however, and the answers can vary in accuracy (some employees are just guessing). Also, to be truly useful, relational data must come from everyone at the company, not just a few people. As an executive at a large financial services company told us, "If I gave each of my 15,000 employees a survey that takes half an hour to do, we've just lost a million dollars in productivity. And what if their relationships change in a month? Will we have to do it again at a cost of an additional $1 million in people hours?"

Company-collected relational data, however, creates new challenges. Although most employment contracts give firms the right to record and monitor activities conducted on company systems, some employees feel that the passive collection of relational data is an invasion of privacy. This is not a trivial concern. Companies need clear HR policies about the gathering and analysis of digital exhaust that help employees understand and feel comfortable with it. (See the sidebar "What About Employee Privacy?")

Behavioral data is a better reflection of reality

As we've noted, digital exhaust is less biased than data collected through surveys. For instance, in surveys people may list connections they think they're supposed to interact with, rather than those they actually do interact with. And because every employee will be on at least several communication platforms, companies can map networks representing the entire workforce, which makes the analysis more accurate.

Also, not all behaviors are equal. Liking someone's post is different from working on a team with someone for two years. Copying someone on an e-mail does not indicate a strong relationship. How all those individual behaviors are weighted and combined matters. This is where machine-learning algorithms and simulation models are helpful. With a little technical know-how (and with an understanding of which structural signatures predict what performance outcomes), setting up those systems is not hard to do.

Constant updating is required

Relationships are dynamic. People and projects come and go. To be useful, relational data must be timely. Using digital exhaust in a relational analytics model addresses that need.

Additionally, collecting relational data over time gives analysts more choices about what to examine. For example, if an employee was out on maternity leave for several months, an analyst can

What about Employee Privacy?

RELATIONAL ANALYTICS CHANGES THE EQUATION when it comes to the privacy of employee data. When employees actively provide information about themselves in hiring forms, surveys, and the like, they know their company has and can use it. But they may not even realize that the passive collection of relational data—such as whom they chat with on Slack or when they were copied on e-mail—is happening or that such information is being analyzed.

Job one for companies is to be transparent. If they're going to amass digital exhaust, they should ask employees to sign an agreement indicating they understand that their patterns of interaction on company-owned tools will be tracked for the purposes of analyzing the organization's social networks. Full disclosure with employee consent is the only option.

We've found some additional moves leaders can make to get ahead of privacy concerns:

First, give employees whatever relational data you collect about them. We recommend providing it at least annually. The data can include a map of the employee's own network and benchmarks. For example, a report could provide an employee with her constraint score (which shows how inbred someone's social network is) and the average constraint score of employees in her department. That score could then be at the center of a mentoring discussion.

Second, be clear about the depth of relational analytics you intend to invest in. The level that is most basic—and the least prone to privacy concerns—is generic pattern analysis. The analysis might show, for example, that marketing is a silo but not identify specific individuals that contribute to that silo. Or the analysis could show that a certain percentage of teams have the signature for innovation but not identify which teams.

The second level identifies which specific employees in a company have certain kinds of networks. Scores may provide evidence-based predictions about employee behavior—such as who is likely to be an influencer or whose departure would make an organization vulnerable. Although this level of analysis provides more value to the company, it singles particular employees out.

The highest level pairs relational analytics with machine learning. In this scenario, companies collect data about whom employees interact with and about the topics they discuss. Firms examine the content of e-mails and posts on social-networking sites to identify who has expertise in what domains. This information provides the most specific guidance for leaders—for example, about who is likely to develop good ideas in certain areas. This most advanced level obviously also comes with the most privacy concerns, and senior leadership must develop deeply considered strategies to deal with them.

exclude that time period from the data or decide to aggregate a larger swath of data. If a company was acquired in a particular year, an analyst can compare relational data from before and after the deal to chart how the company's vulnerabilities may have changed.

Analyses need to be close to decision makers

Most companies rely on data scientists to cull insights related to talent and performance management. That often creates a bottleneck, because there aren't enough data scientists to address all management queries in a timely manner. Plus, data scientists don't know the employees they are running analyses on, so they cannot put results into context.

Dashboards are key

A system that identifies structural signatures and highlights them visually moves analytic insights closer to the managers who need them. As one executive at a semiconductor chip firm told us, "I want my managers to have the data to make good decisions about how to use their employees. And I want them to be able to do it when those decision points happen, not later."

People analytics is a new way to make evidence-based decisions that improve organizations. But in these early days, most companies have been focused on the attributes of individuals, rather than on their relationships with other employees. Looking at attributes will take firms only so far. If they harness relational analytics, however, they can estimate the likelihood that an employee, a team, or an entire organization will achieve a performance goal. They can also use algorithms to tailor staff assignments to changes in employee networks or to a particular managerial need. The best firms, of course, will use relational analytics to augment their own decision criteria and build healthier, happier, and more-productive organizations.

Originally published in November–December 2018. Reprint R1806E

21st-Century Talent Spotting

by Claudio Fernández-Aráoz

A FEW YEARS AGO, I was asked to help find a new CEO for a family-owned electronics retailer that wanted to professionalize its management and expand its operations. I worked closely with the outgoing chief executive and the board to pinpoint the relevant competencies for the job and then seek out and assess candidates. The man we hired had all the right credentials: He'd attended top professional schools and worked for some of the best organizations in the industry, and he was a successful country manager in one of the world's most admired companies. Even more important, he'd scored above the target level for each of the competencies we'd identified. But none of that mattered. Despite his impressive background and great fit, he could not adjust to the massive technological, competitive, and regulatory changes occurring in the market at the time. Following three years of lackluster performance, he was asked to leave.

Compare that story with one from the start of my executive search career. My task was to fill a project manager role at a small brewery owned by Quinsa, which then dominated the beer market in the southern cone of Latin America. In those days, I hadn't yet heard the term "competency." I was working in a new office without research support (in the pre-internet era), and Quinsa was the only serious beverage industry player in the region, so I was simply unable to identify a large pool of people with the right industry and functional background. Ultimately, I contacted Pedro Algorta, an executive I'd met in 1981, while we were both studying at Stanford University. A survivor of the infamous 1972 plane crash in the Andes, which has been chronicled in several books and the movie *Alive*, Algorta was certainly an interesting choice. But he had no experience in the consumer goods business; was unfamiliar with Corrientes, the province where the brewery was located; and had never worked in marketing or sales, key areas of expertise. Still, I had a feeling he would be successful, and Quinsa agreed to hire him. That decision proved to be a smart one. Algorta was rapidly promoted to general manager of the Corrientes brewery and then CEO of Quinsa's flagship Quilmes brewery. He also became a key member of the team that transformed Quinsa from a family-owned enterprise to a large, respected conglomerate with a management team considered at the time to be among the best in Latin America.

Why did the CEO of the electronics business, who seemed so right for the position, fail so miserably? And why did Algorta, so clearly unqualified, succeed so spectacularly? The answer is *potential:* the ability to adapt to and grow into increasingly complex roles and environments. Algorta had it; the first CEO did not.

Having spent 30 years evaluating and tracking executives and studying the factors in their performance, I now consider potential to be the most important predictor of success at all levels, from junior management to the C-suite and the board. I've learned how to identify people who have it and to help companies develop and deploy them. With this article, I share those lessons. As business becomes more volatile and complex, and the global market for top professionals gets tighter, I am convinced that organizations and their leaders must transition to what I think of as a new era of talent spotting—one in which our evaluations of one another are based not on brawn, brains, experience, or competencies, but on potential.

A New Era

The first era of talent spotting lasted millennia. For thousands of years, humans made choices about one another on the basis of

Idea in Brief

The Problem

In the past few decades, organizations have emphasized "competencies" in hiring and developing talent. Jobs have been decomposed into skills and filled by candidates who have them. But 21st-century business is too volatile and complex—and the market for top talent too tight—for that model to work anymore.

The Solution

Today those responsible for hiring and promotion decisions must instead focus on potential: the ability to adapt to ever-changing business environments and grow into challenging new roles.

The Tools

Managers must learn to assess current and prospective employees on five key indicators: the right motivation, curiosity, insight, engagement, and determination. Then they have to help the best get better with smart retention and stretch assignments.

physical attributes. If you wanted to erect a pyramid, dig a canal, fight a war, or harvest a crop, you chose the fittest, healthiest, strongest people you could find. Those attributes were easy to assess, and, despite their growing irrelevance, we still unconsciously look for them: *Fortune* 500 CEOs are on average 2.5 inches taller than the average American, and the statistics on military leaders and country presidents are similar.

I was born and raised during the second era, which emphasized intelligence, experience, and past performance. Throughout much of the 20th century, IQ—verbal, analytical, mathematical, and logical cleverness—was justifiably seen as an important factor in hiring processes (particularly for white-collar roles), with educational pedigrees and tests used as proxies. Much work also became standardized and professionalized. Many kinds of workers could be certified with reliability and transparency, and since most roles were relatively similar across companies and industries, and from year to year, past performance was considered a fine indicator. If you were looking for an engineer, accountant, lawyer, designer, or CEO, you would scout out, interview, and hire the smartest, most experienced engineer, accountant, lawyer, designer, or CEO.

I joined the executive search profession in the 1980s, at the beginning of the third era of talent spotting, which was driven by the competency movement still prevalent today. David McClelland's 1973 paper "Testing for Competence Rather than for 'Intelligence'" proposed that workers, especially managers, be evaluated on specific characteristics and skills that helped predict outstanding performance in the roles for which they were being hired. The time was right for such thinking, because technological evolution and industry convergence had made jobs much more complex, often rendering experience and performance in previous positions irrelevant. So, instead, we decomposed jobs into competencies and looked for candidates with the right combination of them. For leadership roles, we also began to rely on research showing that emotional intelligence was even more important than IQ.

Now we're at the dawn of a fourth era, in which the focus must shift to potential. In a volatile, uncertain, complex, and ambiguous environment (VUCA is the military-acronym-turned-corporate-buzzword), competency-based appraisals and appointments are increasingly insufficient. What makes someone successful in a particular role today might not tomorrow if the competitive environment shifts, the company's strategy changes, or he or she must collaborate with or manage a different group of colleagues. So the question is not whether your company's employees and leaders have the right skills; it's whether they have the potential to learn new ones.

The Scarcity of Top Talent

Unfortunately, potential is much harder to discern than competence (though not impossible, as I'll describe later). Moreover, your organization will be looking for it in what will soon be one of the toughest employment markets in history—for employers, not job seekers. The recent noise about high unemployment rates in the United States and Europe hides important signals: Three forces—globalization, demographics, and pipelines—will make senior talent ever scarcer in the years to come.

Back in 2006, I worked with Nitin Nohria, the current dean of Harvard Business School, and my Egon Zehnder colleagues to study this issue, gathering detailed data and interviewing CEOs from 47 companies with a combined market capitalization of $2 trillion, revenue of over $1 trillion, and more than 3 million employees. Representing all major sectors and geographies, these firms were successful, with strong reputations and solid people practices. Yet we found that all were about to face a massive talent crunch. Eight years later, the situation for companies is just as bad, if not worse.

Let's examine the three factors in turn. *Globalization* compels companies to reach beyond their home markets and to compete for the people who can help them do so. The major global firms in our 2006 study anticipated an 88% increase in their proportion of revenue from developing regions by 2012. Not only did that happen, but the International Monetary Fund and other groups are currently predicting that some 70% of the world's growth between now and 2016 will come from emerging markets. At the same time, firms in developing nations are themselves vying for talent, as well as customers, around the world. Take China, which now has 88 companies in the global *Fortune* 500, up from just eight in 2003, thanks in part to foreign growth. Huawei, the leading Chinese telecommunications company, employs more than 70,000 people, 45% of whom work in R&D centers in countries including Germany, Sweden, the U.S., France, Italy, Russia, and India. Similar examples can be found in companies based in markets such as India and Brazil.

The impact of *demographics* on hiring pools is also undeniable. The sweet spot for rising senior executives is the 35-to-44-year-old age bracket, but the percentage of people in that range is shrinking dramatically. In our 2006 study, we calculated that a projected 30% decline in the ranks of young leaders, combined with anticipated business growth, would cut in half the pool of senior leader candidates in that critical age group. Whereas a decade ago this demographic shift was affecting mostly the United States and Europe, by 2020 many other countries, including Russia, Canada, South Korea, and China, will have more people at retirement age than entering the workforce.

Potential at the Top

A FOCUS ON POTENTIAL can improve talent spotting at every level of the organization—especially the very top. When choosing a CEO or board member, as opposed to a young manager, you'll often find that several candidates have the right credentials, experience, and competencies. That's why an accurate assessment of their motivation, curiosity, insight, engagement, and determination is all the more important.

For CEO roles, succession planning must start very early, ideally when a new leader takes charge but no later than three to four years before he or she expects to leave. At Egon Zehnder, even when a much longer tenure is expected, we help companies assess potential two to four layers below the C-suite, identifying people to retain and develop so that some can become contenders for the top job.

I know one outstanding corporate director who twice orchestrated the dismissal of fully competent C-suite executives because they didn't have enough potential and she wanted to make their roles—key development opportunities—available to people who did. Board appointments require the same discipline. Our firm's UK office recently helped a highly respected retail group, the John Lewis Partnership, evaluate a long list of candidates for two nonexecutive director positions, using all the indicators of potential—curiosity, in particular—as key metrics. After all, if a company's leaders don't have the potential to learn, grow, and adapt to new environments, how can they attract up-and-coming employees and managers who do?

The third phenomenon is related and equally powerful, but much less well known: Companies are not properly developing their *pipelines* of future leaders. In PricewaterhouseCoopers's 2014 survey of CEOs in 68 countries, 63% of respondents said they were concerned about the future availability of key skills at all levels. The Boston Consulting Group cites proprietary research showing that 56% of executives see critical gaps in their ability to fill senior managerial roles in coming years. HBS professor Boris Groysberg found similar concerns in his 2013 survey of executive program participants: Respondents gave their companies' leadership pipelines an average rating of 3.2 out of 5, compared with an average score of 4 for current CEOs and 3.8 for current top teams. Equally troubling were responses to other kinds of questions in the survey: No talent management function was rated higher than 3.3, and critical employee development activities, such as job rotations, were scored as low as 2.6. In other words, few executives think their companies are doing a good job identifying and developing qualified leaders. Recent executive panel interviews conducted by my colleagues confirm that this view is widespread. Only 22% of the 823 leaders who participated consider their pipelines promising, and only 19% said they find it easy to attract the best talent.

In many companies, particularly those based in developed markets, I've found that half of senior leaders will be eligible for retirement within the next two years, and half of them don't have a successor ready or able to take over. As Groysberg puts it, "Companies may not be feeling pain today, but in five or 10 years, as people retire or move on, where will the next generation of leaders come from?"

Taken independently, globalization, demographics, and pipelines would each create unprecedented demand for talent over the next decade. The pace of globalization has never been faster; the imbalance between old and young has never been so dramatic; views on the pipelines of qualified successors have never been more negative; and the survey ratings of development practices are the lowest I've seen. Combine all those factors, and you get a war for talent that will present a huge, perhaps insurmountable, challenge for most organizations. But for those that learn how to spot potential, effectively retain people who have it, and create development programs to help the best get better, the situation will instead offer an extraordinary opportunity.

Better Hiring

The first step is to get the right people into your organization. As Amazon CEO Jeff Bezos, one of the most impressive corporate value creators in recent history, put it in 1998, "Setting the bar high in our approach to hiring has been, and will continue to be, the single most important element of [our] success." So, when evaluating job candidates (and reevaluating current employees), how do you gauge potential?

Many companies have well-established "high potential" programs, through which they fast-track promising managers for development and promotions. But most of these are actually "high performer" programs, full of people who have done well in the past and are therefore assumed to have the best shot of doing well in the future—but given VUCA conditions, that is no longer a safe prediction. About 80% of the participants in the executive programs I teach consistently report that their companies don't use an empirically validated model for assessing potential. I'll admit, this kind of evaluation is much more difficult than measuring IQ, past performance, and even various competencies. But it can be done—with a predictive accuracy around 85%, according to data on the careers of thousands of executives we assessed at Egon Zehnder using a model developed and refined over the past two decades.

The first indicator of potential we look for is the right kind of *motivation:* a fierce commitment to excel in the pursuit of unselfish goals. High potentials have great ambition and want to leave their mark, but they also aspire to big, collective goals, show deep personal humility, and invest in getting better at everything they do. We consider motivation first because it is a stable—and usually unconscious—quality. If someone is driven purely by selfish motives, that probably won't change.

We then consider four other qualities that are hallmarks of potential, according to our research:

- **Curiosity:** a penchant for seeking out new experiences, knowledge, and candid feedback and an openness to learning and change

- **Insight:** the ability to gather and make sense of information that suggests new possibilities

- **Engagement:** a knack for using emotion and logic to communicate a persuasive vision and connect with people

- **Determination:** the wherewithal to fight for difficult goals despite challenges and to bounce back from adversity

In retrospect, I can see that Pedro Algorta succeeded at Quinsa because he had all those qualities, not because he possessed a specific set of skills and competencies. And those qualities were in high relief during his harrowing ordeal in the Andes. He demonstrated his motivation by playing a critical yet humble role—providing sustenance for the explorers who would eventually march out to save the group. He melted snow for them to drink and cut and dried small pieces of flesh from the dead bodies of fellow victims to serve as food. Instead of succumbing to despair, Algorta became curious about the environment around him, taking an interest in the water coming off the ice. It flowed east, leading him, and only him, to the insight that the dying pilot had misreported their position; they were on the Argentine side of the mountain range, not on the Chilean side. His engagement and determination were also clear over those 72 days. He faithfully tended to his dying friend, Arturo Nogueira, who had suffered multiple leg fractures, trying to distract the young man from his pain. He encouraged his fellow survivors to maintain hope and persuaded them all to condone the consumption of their own bodies, should they die, describing it as "an act of love."

Although Algorta's tenure as CEO bears no resemblance to what he experienced on that mountain, the same characteristics served him in his career at Quinsa. Perhaps the best example of the purity of his motives came at the end of his 10-year stint with the company, when, for sound strategic reasons, he recommended that it abandon the agribusiness project he was leading, thus voting himself out of a job. He was also a curious executive, always going out of his way to meet customers, clients, and workers at all levels, and to listen to voices that usually went unheard. As a result, he accepted and supported some revolutionary marketing initiatives, which allowed Quilmes to multiply its sales eightfold while achieving record profitability. He displayed great insight both in his hiring decisions—the future CEOs of both Quilmes and Nestlé were among his best hires—and in his strategic ones: for example, his bold move to divest all noncore assets so that the company could use the proceeds to expand the regional brewery business. His engagement transformed an ineffective and even vicious culture at Quilmes; his insistence that bosses and subordinates come together in open meetings set a precedent that was later rolled out to the whole group. Finally, Algorta showed amazing determination at Quinsa. When the project he'd been hired to lead—the construction of a new brewery—ran out of funds just after he took over, he didn't consider quitting; instead, he pushed to get the necessary financing. And when Argentina was shaken by devaluation and hyperinflation a few months later, he pressed on; the facility was up and running in 15 months.

How can you tell if a candidate you've just met—or a current employee—has potential? By mining his or her personal and professional history, as I've just done with Algorta's. Conduct in-depth interviews or career discussions, and do thorough reference checks to uncover stories that demonstrate whether the person has (or lacks) these qualities. For instance, to assess curiosity, don't just ask, "Are you curious?" Instead, look for signs that the person believes in self-improvement, truly enjoys learning, and is able to recalibrate after missteps. Questions like the following can help:

- How do you react when someone challenges you?

- How do you invite input from others on your team?

- What do you do to broaden your thinking, experience, or personal development?

- How do you foster learning in your organization?

- What steps do you take to seek out the unknown?

Always ask for concrete examples, and go just as deep in your exploration of motivation, insight, engagement, and determination. Your conversations with managers, colleagues, and direct reports who know the person well should be just as detailed.

As a leader, you must also work to spread these interviewing techniques through the organization. Researchers have found that while the best interviewers' assessments have a very high positive correlation with the candidates' ultimate performance, some interviewers' opinions are worse than flipping a coin. Still, few managers learn proper assessment techniques from their business schools or their employers; in my surveys of participants in executive talent management programs, I've found that only about 30% think that their companies provide adequate training. Most organizations, it seems, are filled with people who have the power to endorse bad candidates and kill off good ones.

By contrast, companies that emphasize the right kind of hiring vastly improve their odds. Amazon has, for example, hundreds of dedicated internal recruiters, great training programs in assessment, and even a legion of certified "bar raisers": skilled evaluators who hold full-time jobs in a range of departments but are also empowered to participate in assessing—and vetoing—candidates for other areas.

The Brazilian mining group Companhia Vale do Rio Doce, known as Vale, took a similarly disciplined approach, working with Egon Zehnder, during the 2001 to 2011 tenure of CEO Roger Agnelli. On his watch, not one senior role was filled without an objective, independent, and professional assessment of all internal and external candidates. Managers were encouraged to favor motivated, curious, insightful, engaging, and determined prospects even when they had no specific experience in the field or function to which they had applied. "We would never choose someone who was not passionate and committed to our long-term strategy and demanding objectives," Agnelli explains. Some 250 executives were hired or promoted in this way, all over the world, and the strategy paid off. Vale became a global player in the mining industry, dramatically outperforming others in the country and the region.

Smart Retention

Once you've hired true high potentials and identified the ones you already have, you'll need to focus on keeping them. After all, competitors grappling with the same tight talent market will be more than happy to tempt them away. Agnelli says his proudest achievement at Vale was not the huge revenue, profit, and share price growth over which he presided but the improved quality of the leaders rising through the company's ranks. "After five or six years, everyone appointed at the highest levels came from inside," he says, adding that the capacity to build and retain great teams is *"the* key" to any leader's or organization's success.

Indeed, when the Brazilian government used its 61% stake in Vale's controlling shares to precipitate Agnelli's departure, in 2011, prompting the voluntary resignations of seven out of eight executive committee members within a year, the company soon lost almost half its value. Growing disenchantment with Brazilian and commodity stocks played a role, to be sure. But given that Vale's closest competitors, Rio Tinto and BHP Billiton, saw much less dramatic declines over the same period, it seems clear that investors were also reacting to the loss of an outstanding leadership team.

How can you emulate Vale under Agnelli and avoid the company's subsequent fate? By considering what your high potentials want most from you. As Daniel H. Pink explains in *Drive,* most of us (especially knowledge workers) are energized by three fundamental things: *autonomy*—the freedom to direct our lives; *mastery*—our craving to excel; and *purpose*—the yearning for our work to serve something larger than ourselves.

Pay does matter, of course. All employees, especially rising stars, expect their compensation to reflect their contribution or effort and to be comparable to that of others doing similar jobs. However, in my experience, while unfair pay can surely demotivate, compensation beyond a certain level is much less important than most people think. In my examination of candidates hired through our firm who were successful in their new jobs but moved on within three years, I found that 85% of them were hired away into a more senior position, confirming that they were competent people with potential. But only 4% of them cited more money as the primary reason for their departures. More common reasons were bad bosses, limited support, and lack of opportunities for growth.

So do pay your stars fairly, ideally above the average. But also give them autonomy in four "T" dimensions: task (what they do), time (when they do it), team (whom they do it with), and technique (how they do it). Help them toward mastery by setting difficult but attainable challenges and eliminating distractions. And engage them in a greater team, organizational, or societal goal. Bezos and other leaders at Amazon are expert at this. Agnelli and his team at Vale were, too. But the conditions at the company following his departure failed to motivate the remaining leaders in the same way, and many of them chose to move on.

Stretch Development

Your final job is to make sure your stars live up to the high potential you've spotted in them by offering development opportunities that push them out of their comfort zones. Jonathan Harvey, a top HR executive at ANZ, an Australian bank that operates in 33 countries, puts it this way: "When it comes to developing executives for future leadership assignments, we're constantly striving to find the optimal level of discomfort in the next role or project, because that's where the most learning happens. We don't want people to be stretched beyond their limits. But we want well-rounded, values-focused leaders who see the world through a wide-angle lens, and the right stretch assignments are what helps people get there."

To explain the consequences of *not* challenging your high potentials, I often point to Japan. In 2008 Kentaro Aramaki, from Egon Zehnder's Tokyo office, and I mapped the potential of senior Japanese executives (that is, our consultants' objective assessments of the executives' ability to take on bigger roles and responsibilities, as measured by the indicators described above) against their competence (that is, our objective assessments of the eight leadership competencies listed in the sidebar "What Else Should You Look For?"). When we compared those scores with the average scores of all executives in our worldwide database, we found a great paradox. Japanese professionals had higher potential than the global average but lower competence. In spite of great raw material, there was a poor final product. The problem was, and still is, Japan's flawed development process. Although the country's educational institutions and the strong work ethic that is part of Japanese culture give managers a jump-start in their careers, their growth is stymied when they actually start working. A leader in Japan traditionally rises through

What Else Should You Look For?

Although potential should be the defining measure of executives today, it would be a mistake to ignore other lessons we've learned over the years about how to evaluate people.

Intelligence

Although you probably won't administer an IQ test, it is important to assess a candidate's general intelligence (including analytical, verbal, mathematical, and logical reasoning) by considering educational background, early job experiences, and responses to interview questions. You don't need to look for geniuses; for most jobs anything above a certain level of intelligence has almost no impact on performance. However, you should still hire people clever enough for your requirements, because their general intelligence won't increase dramatically over time.

Values

Values are critical, and you can't expect to impart them on the job. Use interviews and reference checks not only to weigh the essentials, such as honesty and integrity, but also to discover if the candidate shares your organization's core values.

Leadership Abilities

Some competencies are relevant (though not sufficient) when evaluating senior manager candidates. While each job and organization is different, the best leaders have, in some measure, eight abilities.

---

the ranks of one division, in one company, waiting respectfully for promotions that usually come only when he's the most senior person in line for the spot.

Recently a Tokyo-based global conglomerate asked our firm to assess its top dozen senior leaders, all in their mid- to late 50s. This company, which operates in multiple industries and markets, should have been an ideal training ground for executives. However, only one of the managers we evaluated had worked in more than a single business line. The time each had spent working outside Japan was just one year, on average. And their English language skills were quite limited. As a result, none were suitable candidates to succeed the CEO. The

1. **Strategic orientation.** The capacity to engage in broad, complex analytical and conceptual thinking

2. **Market insight.** A strong understanding of the market and how it affects the business

3. **Results orientation.** A commitment to demonstrably improving key business metrics

4. **Customer impact.** A passion for serving the customer

5. **Collaboration and influence.** An ability to work effectively with peers or partners, including those not in the line of command

6. **Organizational development.** A drive to improve the company by attracting and developing top talent

7. **Team leadership.** Success in focusing, aligning, and building effective groups

8. **Change leadership.** The capacity to transform and align an organization around a new goal

You should assess these abilities through interviews and reference checks, in the same way you would evaluate potential, aiming to confirm that the candidate has displayed them in the past, under similar circumstances.

sad thing is that all had started off strong. They were engineers, with an average tenure of more than 20 years in R&D and product strategy and marketing—but that potential had been squandered.

Pushing your high potentials up a straight ladder toward bigger jobs, budgets, and staffs will continue their growth, but it won't accelerate it. Diverse, complex, challenging, uncomfortable roles will. When we recently asked 823 international executives to look back at their careers and tell us what had helped them unleash their potential, the most popular answer, cited by 71%, was stretch assignments. Job rotations and personal mentors, each mentioned by 49% of respondents, tied for second.

How do you make sure people in your organization are getting the stretch assignments and job rotations they need? Let's come back to ANZ. Following a 2007 to 2010 hiring spree as the company expanded across Asia, it decided to refine its leadership development processes. Its efforts center on what it calls business-critical roles: those that make a vital contribution to the strategic agenda; require a scarce set of skills; produce highly variable outcomes dependent on the incumbent; and, if vacant, pose a significant threat to business continuity and performance momentum.

ANZ makes a point of assessing all its managers for potential and then placing those who rate the highest in these business-critical roles. Other development initiatives include the Generalist Bankers Program, which each year offers 10 to 15 participants the opportunity to spend two years rotating through wholesale, commercial, and retail banking, risk, and operations to build broad industry and corporate knowledge. Participants then move into permanent roles with a focus on gaining geographic, cultural, product, and client-facing experience, including a mandatory posting in internal audit to ensure that they understand the bank's control frameworks. The program commitment is 15 years, with the goal of a country CEO posting at the end.

This disciplined approach already seems to be bearing fruit. Whereas three years ago 70% of ANZ's senior executive roles were filled by external candidates, outside hiring is now below 20%. Internal surveys show that staff engagement has increased from 64% to 72%, while "same-period performance excellence" (a measure of employee commitment to customer service and product quality) has jumped from 68% to 78%. And the business has benefited in other ways. In 2013 the company was judged the number four international bank in the Asia Pacific region for the second consecutive year by the highly regarded Greenwich customer survey, up from number 12 in 2008.

Geopolitics, business, industries, and jobs are changing so rapidly that we can't predict the competencies needed to succeed even a few years out. It is therefore imperative to identify and develop people with the highest potential. Look for those who have a strong motivation to excel in the pursuit of challenging goals, along with the humility to put the group ahead of individual needs; an insatiable curiosity that propels them to explore new ideas and avenues; keen insight that allows them to see connections where others don't; a strong engagement with their work and the people around them; and the determination to overcome setbacks and obstacles. That doesn't mean forgetting about factors like intelligence, experience, performance, and specific competencies, particularly the ones related to leadership. But hiring for potential and effectively retaining and developing those who have it—at every level of the organization—should now be your top priority.

Originally published in June 2014. Reprint R1406B

Tours of Duty

The New Employer-Employee Compact.

by Reid Hoffman, Ben Casnocha, and Chris Yeh

FOR MOST OF THE 20TH CENTURY, the compact between employers and employees in the developed world was all about stability. Jobs at big corporations were secure: As long as the company did OK financially and the employee did his or her job, that job wouldn't go away. And in the white-collar world, careers progressed along an escalator of sorts, offering predictable advancement to employees who followed the rules. Corporations, for their part, enjoyed employee loyalty and low turnover.

Then came globalization and the Information Age. Stability gave way to rapid, unpredictable change. Adaptability and entrepreneurship became key to achieving and sustaining success. These changes demolished the traditional employer-employee compact and its accompanying career escalator in the U.S. private sector; they are in varying degrees of disarray elsewhere.

We are not the first to point this out or to propose solutions. But none of the new approaches offered so far have really taken hold. Instead of developing a better compact, many—probably most—companies have tried to become more adaptable by minimizing the existing one. Need to cut costs? Lay off employees. Need new skills? Hire different employees. Under this laissez-faire arrangement, employees are encouraged to think of themselves as "free agents," looking to other companies for opportunities for growth and changing jobs whenever better ones beckon. The result is a winner-take-all economy that may strike top management as fair but generates widespread disillusionment among the rest of the workforce.

Even companies that have succeeded using minimalist compacts experience negative fallout, because the compacts encourage turnover and hamper employee productivity. More important, although the lack of job security indirectly creates incentives for employees to become more adaptable and entrepreneurial, the lack of mutual benefit encourages the most adaptable and entrepreneurial to take their talents elsewhere. The company reaps some cost savings but gains little in the way of innovation and adaptability.

The time has come, we believe, for a new employer-employee compact. You can't have an agile company if you give employees lifetime contracts—and the best people don't want one employer for life anyway. But you can build a better compact than "every man for himself." In fact, some companies are doing so.

We three come from an environment where the employer-employee relationship has already taken new forms—the high-tech start-up community of Silicon Valley. In this world, adaptability and risk taking are acknowledged as crucial to success, and individual entrepreneurs can have a big impact if the networks they've built are strong enough.

Two of us (Reid and Ben) recently wrote a book, *The Start-up of You*, that applied the habits of successful tech entrepreneurs to the work of building a fulfilling career in any field. Obviously, not every industry works like a start-up business. But most firms today operate in a similar environment of rapid change and disruptive innovation.

Tiny start-ups out-execute corporate giants all the time, despite seemingly huge disadvantages in resources and competitive position. Start-ups succeed in large part because their founders, executives, and early employees are highly adaptable, entrepreneurial types who are motivated to out-hustle, out-network, and out-risk their competitors—and who thus generate outsize rewards.

Recruiting, training, and relying on such a workforce can be scary. After all, if you encourage your employees to be entrepreneurial, they might leave you for the competition—or worse, they

Idea in Brief

For most of the 20th century the compact between employers and employees was based on loyalty. That is now gone, replaced in the U.S. by a transactional, laissez-faire approach that serves neither party well.

A workable new compact must recognize that jobs are unlikely to be permanent but encourage lasting alliances nonetheless. The key is that both the employer and the employee seek to add value to each other. Employees invest in the company's *adaptability*; the company invests in employees' *employability*.

Three simple policies can make this new compact tangible. They are (1) hiring employees for explicit "tours of duty," (2) encouraging employees to build networks and expertise outside the organization, and (3) establishing active alumni networks to maintain career-long relationships.

---

might *become* the competition. This is an everyday reality in Silicon Valley. But smart managers here have realized that they can encourage entrepreneurial mind-sets and increase retention by rethinking how they relate to talent within their organizations. What's more, many have come to understand that they can benefit from employees who do leave for other opportunities.

This is the beginning, we think, of the new kind of compact that's needed today. Although it is most evident in the tech world, we've seen elements of it elsewhere—at consulting firms, for example. The chief principle underlying it is reciprocity: Both parties understand and acknowledge that they've entered into a voluntary relationship that benefits both sides.

Mutual investment was implicit in the old lifetime employment compact, to be sure. Because both sides expected the relationship to be permanent, both sides were willing to invest in it. Companies provided training, advancement, and an unspoken guarantee of employment, while employees provided loyalty and a moderation of wage demands. The new compact acknowledges the probable impermanence of the relationship yet seeks to build trust and investment anyway. Instead of entering into strict bonds of loyalty, both sides seek the mutual benefits of *alliance*.

As allies, employer and employee try to add value to each other. The employer says, "If you make us more valuable, we'll make *you* more valuable." The employee says, "If you help me grow and flourish, I'll help the company grow and flourish." Employees invest in the company's *adaptability*; the company invests in employees' *employability*. As former Bain CEO Tom Tierney used to tell recruits and consultants, "We are going to make you more marketable."

The reciprocal compact may be unsentimental, but it depends on trust nonetheless. Because the parties are seeking an alliance rather than just exchanging money for time, it can build a stronger relationship between them even as it acknowledges that relationship's finite life in the organization. This allows both sides to take more risks, investing time and resources to find global maxima rather than simply seeking local peaks.

Netflix's compact with its employees is an example of what these new arrangements can look like. In a famous presentation on his company's culture, CEO Reed Hastings declared, "We're a team, not a family." He gave managers this advice: "Which of my people, if they told me they were leaving in two months for a similar job at a peer company, would I fight hard to keep at Netflix? The other people should get a generous severance now, so we can open a slot to try to find a star for that role." The new compact isn't about being nice. It's based on an understanding that a company is its talent, that low performers will be cut, and that the way to attract talent is to offer appealing opportunities.

We've found three simple, straightforward ways in which organizations have made the new compact tangible and workable. They are (1) hiring employees for defined "tours of duty," (2) encouraging, even subsidizing, the building of employee networks outside the organization, and (3) creating active alumni networks that facilitate career-long relationships between employers and former employees. Let's look at each in turn.

Establishing a "Tour of Duty"

If you think all your people will give you lifetime loyalty, think again: Sooner or later, most employees will pivot into a new opportunity. Recognizing this fact, companies can strike incremental alliances. When Reid founded LinkedIn, he set the initial employee compact as a four-year tour of duty, with a discussion at two years. If an employee moved the needle on the business during the four years, the company would help advance his career. Ideally this would entail another tour of duty at the company, but it could also mean a position elsewhere.

The tour-of-duty approach works: The company gets an engaged employee who's striving to produce tangible achievements for the firm and who can be an important advocate and resource at the end of his tour or tours. The employee may not get lifetime *employment,* but he takes a significant step toward lifetime *employability.* A tour of duty also establishes a realistic zone of trust. Lifelong employment and loyalty are simply not part of today's world; pretending that they are decreases trust by forcing both sides to lie.

Why two to four years? That time period seems to have nearly universal appeal. In the software business, it syncs with a typical product development cycle, allowing an employee to see a major project through. Consumer goods companies such as P&G rotate their brand managers so that each spends two to four years in a particular role. Investment banks and management consultancies have two- to four-year analyst programs. The cycle applies even outside the business world—think of U.S. presidential elections and the Olympics.

Properly implemented, the tour-of-duty approach can boost both recruiting and retention. The key is that it gives employer and employee a clear basis for working together. Both sides agree in advance on the purpose of the relationship, the expected benefits for each, and a planned end.

The problem with most employee retention programs is that they have a fuzzy goal (retain "good" employees) and a fuzzy time frame (indefinitely). Both types of fuzziness destroy trust: The company is asking an employee to commit to it but makes no commitment in return. In contrast, a tour of duty serves as a personalized retention plan that gives a valued employee concrete, compelling reasons to finish her tour and that establishes a clear time frame for discussing the future of the relationship.

Don't Be Afraid of Entrepreneurial Employees

WITH A NEW COMPACT, you can attract entrepreneurial, adaptive people. But relying on entrepreneurial employees can be terrifying: They restlessly search for new, high-learning career opportunities, and other companies are always looking to poach them. Still, it's crucial to have them aboard, even temporarily, so you should put your fears aside. Here's why.

Do entrepreneurial employees really benefit their employers?

They can be extremely valuable, as John Lasseter's story demonstrates. In the early 1980s Lasseter, then a young animator at Disney, pitched his superiors on the new technology of computer-generated animation—and was promptly fired. He ended up in Lucasfilm's computer graphics division, which Steve Jobs acquired and, with Lasseter's help, built into the computer-generated-animation powerhouse Pixar. In 2006 Disney paid $7.4 billion for Pixar and named Lasseter chief creative officer of both Pixar and Walt Disney Animation Studios. Disney learned an expensive lesson: It would have been much cheaper to let Lasseter exercise his creative and entrepreneurial genius in-house.

Quantifying the benefits of entrepreneurial employees is hard, but Global Entrepreneurship Monitor, which studies in-company entrepreneurship, has made some intriguing findings. In a 2011 study it compared the frequency of individuals' "creating and developing new business activities for the organizations they work for" in different nations. It found that "the prevalence of entrepreneurial employee activity as a percentage of the adult population" in economies classified as innovation-driven was more than ten times as high as in factor-driven economies and more than twice as high as in efficiency-driven economies. In other words, entrepreneurial employees are highly correlated with corporate innovation.

If I encourage employees to be entrepreneurial, won't they leave?

Some will. But retaining them for even a limited time can bring enormous benefits.

The Wharton School polls its students about their satisfaction with their pre–business school jobs. It has found that students who came to it from "terminal jobs"—two-year analyst programs, for example—are more positive about their work experience than their

Amazon became a leader in cloud computing thanks to Amazon Web Services, which allows companies to rent storage and computing power rather than having to buy and operate their own servers. The idea for AWS came from Benjamin Black, a website engineering manager at the company, and his manager, Chris Pinkham. In 2003 they realized that the operational expertise that made Amazon an efficient retailer could be repurposed to serve the general market for computing power. They pitched Jeff Bezos on the concept, and after a few iterations Bezos put Pinkham in charge of developing what would become AWS.

Both Black and Pinkham eventually left Amazon to start their own companies. But they left behind a business unit that contributed some $2 billion to Amazon's revenue in 2012.

Won't tours of duty shorten employee tenure?

A tour of duty has a defined end, but that doesn't have to be the end of an employee's tenure. One successful tour is likely to lead to another. Each strengthens the bonds of trust and mutual benefit. And if an employee wants change, an appealing new tour of duty can provide it within your company rather than at a competitor. This is a more effective retention strategy than appealing to vague notions of loyalty.

Do *all* my employees need to be entrepreneurial?

You don't need or even want 100% of your employees to be hard-core entrepreneurs. Silicon Valley start-ups like to brag about hiring "rock stars," but a company composed of only rock stars would be a nightmare. Every company needs a mix of types that's appropriate for its competitive environment. Companies in relatively stable industries, for example, may do best with fewer entrepreneurial employees.

Still, the chances that your organization is *too* entrepreneurial are pretty low.

peers are. Terminal jobs are generic versions of tours of duty; personalized tours would probably produce even more positive feelings.

In 2003 Matt Cohler was a management consultant who wanted to become a venture capitalist, although he lacked start-up experience.

He began working for Reid at LinkedIn, where the two mapped out a two-year tour of duty. After that time was up, he and Reid agreed to extend the tour while they figured out what Matt could do next. Six months later Matt had the opportunity to join Facebook as one of its first five employees. Although Reid didn't want to lose Matt, he advised him to take the position, which would bring diversity to his start-up experience and move him closer to his goal. After three years at Facebook Matt became the youngest general partner at Benchmark, a prominent venture capital firm.

Action item: Construct personalized, mutually beneficial tours

Work with key employees to establish explicit terms of their tours of duty, developing firm but time-limited mutual commitments with focused goals and clear expectations. Ask, "In this alliance, how will both parties benefit and progress?"

When possible, a tour of duty should offer an employee the possibility of a breakout entrepreneurial opportunity. This might involve building and launching a new product, reengineering an existing business process, or introducing an organizational innovation.

This approach can't be executed by a central HR function; you're making a compact, not drawing up a contract. We're not suggesting that you negotiate a guaranteed arrangement that spells out all the specifics—a rigid approach is the opposite of an entrepreneurial mind-set. You're building a trust relationship that's based on the employee's actual job, so the conversations must be handled by direct managers.

Engaging Beyond the Company's Boundaries

Henry Ford once complained, "Why is it that every time I ask for a pair of hands, they come with a mind attached?" But these days, of course, minds dramatically amplify the value of hands—and they become even more powerful when they're able to engage with minds outside the company.

No matter how many smart employees you have, there are always more smart people outside your company than within it. This is true of all organizations, from one-person start-ups to the Googles of the world.

You can engage with smart minds outside your company through the network intelligence of your employees. The wider an employee's network, the more he or she will be able to contribute to innovation. Martin Ruef, of Duke University, has found that entrepreneurs with diverse friends scored three times as high as others on measures of innovation. To maximize diversity and thus innovation, you need networks both inside and outside your company.

Therefore, employers should encourage employees to build and maintain professional networks that involve the outside world. Essentially, you want to tell your workers, "We will provide you with time to build your network and will pay for you to attend events where you can extend it. In exchange, we ask that you leverage that network to help the company." This is a great example of mutual trust and investment: You're trusting your employees by giving them the resources to build their networks, and they're investing in your business by deploying some of their relationship capital in your company's behalf.

Those networks should encompass the entire environment in which your business operates, including customers and competitors alike and serving as platforms for information on new technology and other trends. For example, at the venture capital firm Greylock, where Reid is a partner, tapping the investment professionals' external networks is an important part of product review meetings. Someone might ask, "What new technologies are you hearing about? Which ones should we investigate?" The insights gained translate into better decision making and more value for Greylock's portfolio companies. The partners at another top venture capital firm, Andreessen Horowitz, have their own creative spin: At the beginning of every meeting, they award a cash prize for the best industry rumor someone has heard. You don't have to be in venture capital to adapt such techniques for your company.

The power of external engagement helped define the history of Silicon Valley high tech, as chronicled in AnnaLee Saxenian's 1994 book on technology clusters, *Regional Advantage*. In 1970 some of the world's largest technology firms were located in Boston's Route 128 corridor. Today none of the 10 largest tech firms are; Boston's primacy has been snatched away by Silicon Valley. What made that possible? External networks.

Massachusetts companies typically preferred secrecy to openness and rigorously enforced noncompete clauses to prevent employees from jumping to rival firms or starting their own. Silicon Valley has long had a more open culture (and lacks enforceable noncompete clauses), and this has permitted the development of much denser and more highly interconnected networks—which make it easier for people to innovate. The area even gave rise to a term, "coopetition," that reflects the fact that working with competitors can be mutually beneficial. Consider Netflix again: It runs its streaming video service on Amazon's cloud platform, even though Amazon's Instant Video is a direct competitor.

Action item: Encourage network development

In *The Start-up of You* we wrote, "Your career success depends on both your individual capabilities and your network's ability to magnify them. Think of it as I^{We}. An individual's power is raised exponentially with the help of a team (a network)."

Just as an individual's power rises with the strength of her network (I^{We}), a company's power rises with the strength of its employees' networks. Value each person's network and her ability to tap it for intelligence; make it an explicit, acknowledged asset. An employee who keeps her LinkedIn profile current or builds a big personal following on Twitter is doing right by your company, not being disloyal to it. And make a candidate's network strength and diversity a priority when hiring. Bringing in employees with strong networks is good; hiring people whose networks complement rather than overlap those of existing employees is even better.

One of the techniques we recommend for individuals is to maintain an "interesting-person fund" to take people in their networks out to coffee. The corporate equivalent is a "networking fund" for employees. To make sure your company reaps the full benefits, establish two requirements for tapping the fund. First, employees have to leave your corporate campus; you want them to get "outside the building" to build a more diverse external network. Second, they must report back about what they learn so that the gains are shared. Most companies allow employees to expense business lunches, but few allow them to expense networking lunches. Yet if you're a top executive, you probably have such lunches all the time, and your company benefits as a result. Make it not just acceptable but *expected* for your people to do the same.

HubSpot, a Massachusetts-based marketing software company that, in its words, believes in "invest[ing] in [the] individual mastery and market value" of every HubSpotter, keeps it even simpler than that. Interested in a book? Mention it on the internal company wiki, and the book will show up on your Kindle. Want to take somebody smart to lunch? Company policy is: "Expense it. No approval needed."

The network intelligence flowing into your company needs to be a top management concern, with specific programs to strengthen and extend it. For highly networked and entrepreneurial employees, this is one of the primary criteria for judging your attractiveness as an employer.

Building Alumni Networks

The first thing you should do when a valuable employee tells you he is leaving is try to change his mind. The second is congratulate him on the new job and welcome him to your company's alumni network.

Just because a job ends, your relationship with your employee doesn't have to. Corporate alumni networks are a prime way to maintain long-term relationships with your best people. As Cindy Lewiton Jackson noted while she was the global director of career development and alumni relations at Bain, "The goal is not to retain employees. The goal is to build lifelong affiliation."

Some industries and firms have long understood this. McKinsey & Company has operated an alumni network since the 1960s; the group now has upwards of 24,000 members (including more than 230 CEOs of companies with at least $1 billion in annual revenue). Booz Allen Hamilton's network has 38,000 people.

One obvious benefit of alumni networks is the opportunity to rehire former employees. The Corporate Executive Board reports that rolling out the CEB Alumni Network doubled its rehire rate in just two years. But the value goes far beyond that. Your alumni are among your most effective means of external engagement. They can share competitive information, effective business practices, emerging industry trends, and more. They understand how your organization works and are generally inclined to help you if they can. Bain's Tom Tierney has observed, "Our number one source of high-quality new business is our alumni."

It may be that management consultancies have pioneered corporate alumni networks because the organizational practices of those firms (two-year analyst programs, "up or out" advancement, encouragement of consultants to take positions with clients) align so well with the concept—but the practice is spreading. LinkedIn now hosts thousands of corporate alumni groups, including those of 98% of the *Fortune* 500 companies. Such groups are often informal, not official; they spring up because alumni want to stay in touch with and help one another. In a study from the University of Twente, in the Netherlands, only 15% of the companies surveyed had official alumni networks, but 67% had independently organized, informal groups.

You might fear that running an alumni network is an admission of failure—a sign that your company can't retain its best people. But your alumni are likely to form a network anyway; the only real question is whether your company will have a voice in it. Alumni are fallow resources waiting for you to tap them. So why don't you?

Action item: Utilize your exit interviews
The traditional exit interview represents a lost opportunity. Instead of collecting perfunctory feedback that they'll probably just ignore, your managers should gather information that can help

you maintain long-term relationships with departing employees (and induct them into your alumni network!). Keep a database of information on all former employees: personal e-mail and phone, LinkedIn profile, Twitter handle, blog URL, areas of expertise, and so on.

The exit interview is also a trust-building opportunity. Many employees have sat through grimly polite or even resentful parting talks. You can make your company stand out by emphasizing the ongoing nature of the relationship. This is also, of course, an opportunity to learn about ways the company and you can do better. Departing employees are more likely than current ones to be honest, and the flaws in your business and organizational practices may be on their minds. Listen closely to what they say.

If the employee who's leaving is one of your stars, you should provide an even higher level of service (assuming he handles his departure professionally and doesn't take the rest of the organization with him). Such folks are likely to go on to great things and to be the hubs of their networks, which could prove very valuable to you. As with the tour of duty, aim for a two-way flow of value; you need to provide benefits if you expect to receive them. The benefits you offer may depend on the business you're in. For example, management consultancies often give free insights to alumni who have joined industry clients. If you're a consumer company, offer alumni discounts in addition to the customary employee discounts. The cost is minimal, and the trust and goodwill gained can be substantial. Some might consider it extravagant to "reward" employees who have left, but that view misses the point. Most employees don't leave because they're disloyal; they leave because you can't match the opportunity offered by another company.

If you don't have the resources to set up a formal alumni network, you can support the informal networks that arise on LinkedIn or Facebook. Your assistance can cover the gamut, from giving financial rewards to alumni who help your firm to handing out company swag or paying for pizza during a meetup. Even distributing an alumni newsletter can contribute to an ongoing cordial relationship at practically no cost.

The Virtuous Circle

An employee who is networking energetically, keeping her LinkedIn profile up to date, and thinking about other opportunities is *not* a liability. In fact, such entrepreneurial, outward-oriented, forward-looking people are probably just what your company needs more of.

How do you square the need for such people with the reality that many of them won't stick around forever? First, by accepting that reality. A CEB study of 20,000 workers identified by their employers as "high potentials" found that one in four of them planned to be working elsewhere within the year (see "How to Keep Your Top Talent," HBR May 2010). Once you get past this scary truth, you'll find it easier to achieve honest, productive relationships that support your employees' ambitions. This will make your employees more effective on the job and may actually keep them around longer.

The key to the new employer-employee compact we envision is that although it's not based on loyalty, it's not purely transactional, either. It's an alliance between an organization and an individual that's aimed at helping both succeed.

In the war for talent, such a pact can be the secret weapon that helps you fill your ranks with the creative, adaptive superstars everyone wants. These are the entrepreneurial employees who drive business success—and business success makes you even more attractive to entrepreneurial employees. This virtuous circle has created a competitive advantage in talent for Silicon Valley companies. It can work for your company, too.

Originally published in June 2013. Reprint R1306B

Creating the Best Workplace on Earth

by Rob Goffee and Gareth Jones

SUPPOSE YOU WANT TO DESIGN the best company on earth to work for. What would it be like? For three years we've been investigating this question by asking hundreds of executives in surveys and in seminars all over the world to describe their ideal organization. This mission arose from our research into the relationship between authenticity and effective leadership. Simply put, people will not follow a leader they feel is inauthentic. But the executives we questioned made it clear that to be authentic, they needed to work for an authentic organization.

What did they mean? Many of their answers were highly specific, of course. But underlying the differences of circumstance, industry, and individual ambition we found six common imperatives. Together they describe an organization that operates at its fullest potential by allowing people to do their best work.

We call this "the organization of your dreams." In a nutshell, it's a company where individual differences are nurtured; information is not suppressed or spun; the company adds value to employees, rather than merely extracting it from them; the organization stands for something meaningful; the work itself is intrinsically rewarding; and there are no stupid rules.

These principles might all sound commonsensical. Who wouldn't want to work in a place that follows them? Executives are certainly aware of the benefits, which many studies have confirmed. Take these two examples: Research from the Hay Group finds that highly engaged employees are, on average, 50% more likely to exceed expectations than the least-engaged workers. And companies with highly engaged people outperform firms with the most disengaged folks—by 54% in employee retention, by 89% in customer satisfaction, and by fourfold in revenue growth. Recent research by our London Business School colleague Dan Cable shows that employees who feel welcome to express their authentic selves at work exhibit higher levels of organizational commitment, individual performance, and propensity to help others.

Yet, few, if any, organizations possess all six virtues. Several of the attributes run counter to traditional practices and ingrained habits. Others are, frankly, complicated and can be costly to implement. Some conflict with one another. Almost all require leaders to carefully balance competing interests and to rethink how they allocate their time and attention.

So the company of your dreams remains largely aspirational. We offer our findings, therefore, as a challenge: an agenda for leaders and organizations that aim to create the most productive and rewarding working environment possible.

Let People Be Themselves

When companies try to accommodate differences, they too often confine themselves to traditional diversity categories—gender, race, age, ethnicity, and the like. These efforts are laudable, but the executives we interviewed were after something more subtle—differences in perspectives, habits of mind, and core assumptions.

The vice chancellor at one of the world's leading universities, for instance, would walk around campus late at night to locate the research hot spots. A tough-minded physicist, he expected to find them in the science labs. But much to his surprise, he discovered them in all kinds of academic disciplines—ancient history, drama, the Spanish department.

Idea in Brief

You want to design the best company on earth to work for. What would it be like? The response from hundreds of executives all over the world, in a nutshell, is that their dream organization is a place where:

- You can be yourself.
- You're told what's really going on.
- Your strengths are magnified.
- The company stands for something meaningful.
- Your daily work is rewarding.
- Stupid rules don't exist.

Those virtues seem like common sense, but few companies exemplify all six. Some of the attributes conflict, and many are complicated, costly, or time-consuming to implement. Almost all of them require leaders to carefully balance competing interests and reallocate their time and attention. So the list stands as a challenge: It's an agenda for executives who aim to create the most productive and rewarding working environment possible.

The ideal organization is aware of dominant currents in its culture, work habits, dress code, traditions, and governing assumptions but, like the chancellor, makes explicit efforts to transcend them. We are talking not just about the buttoned-down financial services company that embraces the IT guys in shorts and sandals, but also the hipster organization that doesn't look askance when someone wears a suit. Or the place where nearly everyone comes in at odd hours but that accommodates the one or two people who prefer a 9-to-5 schedule.

For example, at LVMH, the world's largest luxury-goods company (and growing rapidly), you'd expect to find brilliant, creative innovators like Marc Jacobs and Phoebe Philo. And you do. But alongside them you also encounter a higher-than-expected proportion of executives and specialists who monitor and assess ideas with an analytical business focus. One of the ingredients in LVMH's success is having a culture where opposite types can thrive and work cooperatively. Careful selection is part of the secret: LVMH looks for creative people who want their designs to be marketable and who, in turn, are more likely to appreciate monitors who are skilled at spotting commercial potential.

The benefits of tapping the full range of people's knowledge and talents may be obvious, yet it's not surprising that so few companies do it. For one thing, uncovering biases isn't easy. (Consider the assumption the diligent chancellor made when he equated research intensity with late-night lab work.) More fundamentally, though, efforts to nurture individuality run up against countervailing efforts to increase organizational effectiveness by forging clear incentive systems and career paths. Competence models, appraisal systems, management by objectives, and tightly defined recruitment policies all narrow the range of acceptable behavior.

Companies that succeed in nurturing individuality, therefore, may have to forgo some degree of organizational orderliness. Take Arup, perhaps the world's most creative engineering and design company. Many iconic buildings bear the mark of Arup's distinctive imprint—from the Sydney Opera House to the Centre Pompidou to the Beijing Water Cube.

Arup approaches its work holistically. When the firm builds a suspension bridge, for example, it looks beyond the concerns of the immediate client to the region that relies on the bridge. To do so, Arup's people collaborate with mathematicians, economists, artists, and politicians alike. Accordingly, Arup considers the capacity to absorb different skill sets and personalities as key to its strategy. "We want there to be interesting parts that don't quite fit in . . . that take us places where we didn't expect to get to," says chairman Philip Dilley. "That's part of my job now—to prevent it from becoming totally orderly."

Conventional appraisal systems don't work in such a world, so Arup doesn't use quantitative performance-measurement systems or articulate a corporate policy on how employees should progress. Managers make their expectations clear, but individuals decide how to meet them. "Self-determination means setting your own path and being accountable for your success," a senior HR official explains. "Development and progression is your own business, with our support."

If this sounds too chaotic for a more conventional company, consider Waitrose, one of Britain's most successful food retailers, according to measures as diverse as market share, profitability, and customer and staff loyalty. In an industry that necessarily focuses on executing processes efficiently, Waitrose sees its competitive edge in nurturing the small sparks of creativity that make a big difference to the customer experience.

Waitrose is a cooperative: Every employee is a co-owner who shares in the company's annual profits. So the source of staff loyalty is not much of a mystery. But even so, the company goes to great lengths to draw out and support people's personal interests. If you want to learn piano, Waitrose will pay half the cost of the lessons. There's a thriving club culture—cooking, crafts, swimming, and so on. We have a friend whose father learned to sail because he worked for this organization. In that way, Waitrose strives to create an atmosphere where people feel comfortable being themselves. We were struck when a senior executive told us, "Friends and family would recognize me at work."

"Great retail businesses depend on characters who do things a bit differently," another executive explained. "Over the years we have had lots of them. We must be careful to cherish them and make sure our systems don't squeeze them out."

Pursuit of predictability leads to a culture of conformity, what Emile Durkheim called "mechanical solidarity." But companies like LVMH, Arup, and Waitrose are forged out of "organic solidarity"— which, Durkheim argued, rests on the productive exploitation of differences. Why go to all the trouble? We think Ted Mathas, head of the mutual insurance company New York Life, explains it best: "When I was appointed CEO, my biggest concern was, would this [job] allow me to truly say what I think? I needed to be myself to do a good job. Everybody does."

Unleash the Flow of Information

The organization of your dreams does not deceive, stonewall, distort, or spin. It recognizes that in the age of Facebook, WikiLeaks, and Twitter, you're better off telling people the truth before someone else does. It respects its employees' need to know what's really going on

The "Dream Company" Diagnostic

HOW CLOSE IS YOUR ORGANIZATION to the ideal? To find out, check off each statement that applies. The more checkmarks you have, the closer you are to the dream.

Let Me Be Myself

☐ I'm the same person at home as I am at work.

☐ I feel comfortable being myself.

☐ We're all encouraged to express our differences.

☐ People who think differently from most do well here.

☐ Passion is encouraged, even when it leads to conflict.

☐ More than one type of person fits in here.

Tell Me What's Really Going On

☐ We're all told the whole story.

☐ Information is not spun.

☐ It's not disloyal to say something negative.

☐ My manager wants to hear bad news.

☐ Top executives want to hear bad news.

☐ Many channels of communication are available to us.

☐ I feel comfortable signing my name to comments I make.

Discover and Magnify My Strengths

☐ I am given the chance to develop.

☐ Every employee is given the chance to develop.

☐ The best people want to strut their stuff here.

☐ The weakest performers can see a path to improvement.

☐ Compensation is fairly distributed throughout the organization.

---

so that they can do their jobs, particularly in volatile environments where it's already difficult to keep everyone aligned and where workers at all levels are being asked to think more strategically. You'd imagine that would be self-evident to managers everywhere. In reality, the

☐ We generate value for ourselves by adding value to others.

Make Me Proud I Work Here

☐ I know what we stand for.

☐ I value what we stand for.

☐ I want to exceed my current duties.

☐ Profit is not our overriding goal.

☐ I am accomplishing something worthwhile.

☐ I like to tell people where I work.

Make My Work Meaningful

☐ My job is meaningful to me.

☐ My duties make sense to me.

☐ My work gives me energy and pleasure.

☐ I understand how my job fits with everyone else's.

☐ Everyone's job is necessary.

☐ At work we share a common cause.

Don't Hinder Me with Stupid Rules

☐ We keep things simple.

☐ The rules are clear and apply equally to everyone.

☐ I know what the rules are for.

☐ Everyone knows what the rules are for.

☐ We, as an organization, resist red tape.

☐ Authority is respected.

barriers to what we call "radical honesty"—that is, entirely candid, complete, clear, and timely communication—are legion.

Some managers see parceling out information on a need-to-know basis as important to maintaining efficiency. Others practice a seemingly benign type of paternalism, reluctant to worry staff with certain information or to identify a problem before having a solution. Some feel an obligation to put a positive spin on even the most negative situations out of a best-foot-forward sense of loyalty to the organization.

The reluctance to be the bearer of bad news is deeply human, and many top executives well know that this tendency can strangle the flow of critical information. Take Novo Nordisk's Mads Øvlisen, who was CEO in the 1990s, when violations of FDA regulations at the company's Danish insulin-production facilities became so serious that U.S. regulators nearly banned the insulin from the U.S. market. Incredible as it seems in hindsight, no one told Øvlisen about the situation. That's because Novo Nordisk operated under a culture in which the executive management board was never supposed to receive bad news.

The company took formal steps to rectify the situation, redesigning the company's entire quality-management system—its processes, procedures, and training of all involved personnel. Eventually, those practices were extended to new-product development, manufacturing, distribution, sales, and support systems. More generally, a vision, core values, and a set of management principles were explicitly articulated as the Novo Nordisk Way. To get at the root cause of the crisis, Øvlisen also set out to create a new culture of honesty through a process he called "organizational facilitation"— that is, facilitation of the flow of honest information.

A core team of facilitators (internal management auditors) with long organizational experience now regularly visit all of the company's worldwide affiliates. They interview randomly selected employees and managers to assess whether the Novo Nordisk Way is being practiced. Employees know, for instance, that they must inform all stakeholders both within and outside the organization of what's happening, even when something goes wrong, as quickly as possible. Does this really happen? Many employees have told us that they appreciate these site visits because they foster honest conversations about fundamental business values and processes.

Radical honesty is not easy to implement. It requires opening many different communication channels, which can be time-consuming to maintain. And for previously insulated top managers, it can be somewhat ego-bruising. Witness what ensued when Novo Nordisk recently banned soda from all its buildings. PeopleCom, the company's internal news site, was flooded with hundreds of passionate responses. Some people saw it as an attack on personal freedom. ("I wonder what will be the next thing NN will 'help' me not to do," wrote one exasperated employee. "Ban fresh fruit in an effort to reduce sugar consumption?") Others defended the policy as a logical extension of the company's focus on diabetes. ("We can still purchase our own sugary soft drinks . . . Novo Nordisk shouldn't be a 7-Eleven.") That all these comments were signed indicates how much honesty has infused Novo Nordisk's culture.

Trade secrets will always require confidentiality. And we don't want to suggest that honesty will necessarily stop problems from arising, particularly in highly regulated industries that routinely find themselves under scrutiny. We maintain, though, that executives should err on the side of transparency far more than their instincts suggest. Particularly today, when trust levels among both employees and customers are so low and background noise is so high, organizations must work very hard to communicate what's going on if they are to be heard and believed.

Magnify People's Strengths

The ideal company makes its best employees even better—and the least of them better than they ever thought they could be. In robust economies, when competition for talent is fierce, it's easy to see that the benefits of developing existing staff outweigh the costs of finding new workers. But even then, companies grumble about losing their investment when people decamp for more-promising opportunities. In both good times and bad, managers are far more often rewarded for minimizing labor costs than for the longer-term goal of increasing workers' effectiveness. Perhaps that explains why this aspiration, while so widely recognized and well understood, often remains unfulfilled.

Elite universities and hospitals, Goldman Sachs and McKinsey, and design firms like Arup have all been adding value to valuable people for a very long time. Google and Apple are more recent examples. They do this in myriad ways—by providing networks, creative interaction with peers, stretch assignments, training, and a brand that confers elite status on employees. None of this is rocket science, nor is it likely to be news to anyone.

But the challenge of finding, training, and retaining excellent workers is not confined to specialized, high-tech, or high-finance industries. We contend that the employee-employer relationship is shifting in many industries from how much value can be extracted from workers to how much can be instilled in them. At heart, that's what productivity improvement really means.

Take McDonald's, a company founded on the primacy of cost efficiency. In an economy with plenty of people looking for jobs, McDonald's nevertheless focuses on the growth paths of its front-line workers—and on a large scale. In the UK, the company invests £36 million ($55 million) a year in giving its 87,500 employees the chance to gain a wide range of nationally recognized academic qualifications while they work. One of the largest apprenticeship providers in the country, McDonald's has awarded more than 35,000 such qualifications to employees since the program's launch in 2006. Every week the equivalent of six full classes of students acquire formal credentials in math and English. Every day another 20 employees earn an apprenticeship qualification.

Like many large companies, McDonald's has extensive management training programs for its executives, but the firm also extends that effort to restaurant general managers, department managers, and shift managers who, as the day-to-day leaders on the front lines, are taught the communication and coaching skills they need to motivate crews and to hit their shifts' sales targets. The return on the company's investment is measured not in terms of increased revenue or profitability but in lower turnover of hourly managers and their crews. Turnover has declined steadily since the programs were initiated, as reflected in the Great Place to Work Institute's recognition of McDonald's as one of the 50 best workplaces every year since 2007.

To get a sense of how far employee development can be taken, consider Games Makers, the volunteer training effort mounted by the London Organising Committee of the Olympic Games. LOCOG was responsible for the largest peacetime workforce ever assembled in the UK. It coordinated the activities of more than 100,000 subcontractors, 70,000 Games Makers volunteers, and 8,000 paid staff. Games Makers used bold, imaginative schemes to employ people who had never worked or volunteered before. Through its Trailblazer program, for example, paid staff learned how to work effectively with volunteers of all social backgrounds. Through a partnership with other state agencies, the Personal Best program enabled more than 7,500 disadvantaged, long-term-unemployed individuals, some with physical or learning disabilities, to earn a job qualification. Games Makers' School Leavers program targeted students who have left school in east London, the host borough for the games, by granting them two three-month placements that, upon successful completion, were followed by a contract for employment until the end of the event. LOCOG's model has inspired government agencies and private-sector employment bureaus in the UK to rewrite their work-engagement guidelines to enable them to tap into—and make productive—a far wider range of people than had previously been considered employable.

We recognize that promising to bring out the best in everyone is a high-risk, high-reward strategy. It raises reputational capital, and such capital is easily destroyed. Goldman Sachs, for one, spent years building its reputation as the most exciting investment bank of all. That's why Greg Smith's scathing resignation letter, accusing the company of not living up to its own standards, was so damaging. Once a company heads down this road, it has to keep going.

Stand for More Than Shareholder Value

People want to be a part of something bigger than themselves, something they can believe in. "I've worked in organizations where people try to brainwash me about the virtues of the brand," one seminar participant told us. "I want to work in an organization where I can really feel where the company comes from and what it stands for so that I can live the brand."

It has become commonplace to assert that organizations need shared meaning, and this is surely so. But shared meaning is about more than fulfilling your mission statement—it's about forging and maintaining powerful connections between personal and organizational values. When you do that, you foster individuality and a strong culture at the same time.

Some people might argue that certain companies have an inherent advantage in this area. An academic colleague once asked us if we were working with anyone interesting. When we mentioned Novo Nordisk, he produced from his briefcase a set of Novo pens for injecting insulin and said simply, "They save my life every day." Engineers who design the side bars for BMW's mini have been known to wake up at 4:00 in the morning to write down ideas that will make the cars safer. And that might be expected of people drawn to the idea of building "the ultimate driving machine."

But the advantage these companies have is not the businesses they're in. The connections they forge stem, rather, from the way they do business. To understand how that works more generally, consider Michael Barry, who once was a teacher made redundant by state spending cuts. Three decades later, the experience remained vividly traumatic: "It was a case of 'last in, first out,' nothing to do with merit. I decided I never wanted to lose my job like that again. I researched things quite carefully, looking for places that were clear about what they wanted."

And where did this idealistic man go? He became an insurance salesman for New York Life. "It is a very different company—from the top down," he said, when we asked him what connection he felt to the company. He further explained it this way: "Back when other life insurance companies were demutualizing and becoming financial services supermarkets, New York Life made it very clear that life insurance would remain our core focus. The agents didn't like it [at first]—they felt they were losing the opportunity to make more money. But Sy Sternberg, the CEO at that time, went to public forums with the agents and pulled no punches. He told us, 'We are a life insurance company, and we are good at it.'" This is more than a business strategy, Barry says. "It's how we operate every day. This is not a place where we wriggle out of claims. One man took out a life policy, went home to write out the check. It was on his desk when he died that night. The policy was unpaid, but we paid the claim. The agents really buy into this."

Current CEO Ted Mathas acknowledges that New York Life's status as a mutual company gives it an advantage in claiming that profit is not all that matters. But he argues that the same logic applies for public firms—that profit is (or should be) an outcome of the pursuit of other, more meaningful goals. Again, this is hardly a new idea. "But many companies in public ownership have lost their way and with it a sense of who they are," Mathas suggests, and we agree.

Show How the Daily Work Makes Sense

Beyond shared meaning, the executives we've spoken to want something else. They seek to derive meaning from their daily activities.

This aspiration cannot be fulfilled in any comprehensive way through job enrichment add-on. It requires nothing less than a deliberate reconsideration of the tasks each person is performing. Do those duties make sense? Why are they what they are? Are they as engaging as they can be? This is a huge, complex undertaking.

Take John Lewis, the parent company of Waitrose and the department store Peter Jones. In 2012 it completed a review of its more than 2,200 jobs, slotting them within a hierarchy of 10 levels, to make it easier for employees to take advantage of opportunities across the organization. This sounds like a homogenizing move, and it might be at a traditional company. But at John Lewis, which operates for the benefit of its employee owners, it was a deliberate effort to match its people with the work they want to do.

Or consider Rabobank Nederland, the banking arm of the largest financial services provider in the Netherlands, Rabobank Group. After several years of development, the bank has rolled out Rabo Unplugged, an organizational and technical infrastructure that allows employees to connect to one another from practically anywhere while still meeting the stringent encryption standards that banking systems require. With no fixed offices or rigid job descriptions, Rabobank's employees are, like Arup's, responsible for the results of their work. But they are free to choose how, where, when, and with whom to carry it out. This approach requires managers to place an extraordinary amount of trust in subordinates, and it demands that employees become more entrepreneurial and collaborative.

Beyond reconsidering individual roles, making work rewarding may mean rethinking the way companies are led. Arup's organization, which might be described as "extreme seamless," is one possible model. As such, it takes some getting used to. In describing how this works in Arup's Associates unit, board member Tristram Carfrae explains: "We have architects, engineers, quantity surveyors, and project managers in the same room together . . . people who genuinely want to submerge their own egos into the collective and not [be led] in the classic sense." That was a challenge for Carfrae, who as a structural engineer wrestled with the question of when to impose his will on the team and push it toward a structural, rather than a mechanical or an architecturally oriented, solution. To participate in such an evenhanded, interdependent environment is extremely hard, he says. There were "incredible rewards when it worked well and incredible frustrations when it didn't."

We don't wish to underplay this challenge. But we suggest that the benefits of rising to it are potentially very great. Where work is meaningful, it typically becomes a cause, as it is for the engineers at BMW and the agents at New York Life. We also acknowledge an element of risk: When we interviewed legendary games designer Will Wright, he told us that his primary loyalty was not to his company, Electronic Arts, but to the project—originally for him the record-breaking Sims franchise and, more recently, Spore. Will ultimately left EA to start his own company, in which EA became a joint investor.

The challenge is similar to that of fostering personal growth. If you don't do it, the best people may leave or never consider you at all. Or your competitors may develop the potential in people you've overlooked. When you do make the investment, your staff members become more valuable to you and your competitors alike. The trick, then, is to make it meaningful for them to stay.

Have Rules People Can Believe In

No one should be surprised that, for many people, the dream organization is free of arbitrary restrictions. But it does not obliterate all rules. Engineers, even at Arup, must follow procedures and tight quality controls—or buildings will collapse.

Organizations need structure. Markets and enterprises need rules. As successful entrepreneurial businesses grow, they often come to believe that new, complicated processes will undermine their culture. But systematization need not lead to bureaucratization, not if people understand what the rules are for and view them as legitimate. Take Vestergaard Frandsen, a start-up social enterprise that makes mosquito netting for the developing world. The company is mastering the art of behavior codes that can help structure its growing operations without jeopardizing its culture. Hiring (and firing) decisions are intentionally simple—only one level of approval is required for each position. Regional directors have significant freedom within clear deadlines and top- and bottom-line targets. Knowledge-management systems are designed to encourage people to call rather than e-mail one another and to explain why someone is being cc'ed on an e-mail message. Vestergaard sees these simple rules as safeguards rather than threats to its founding values.

Despite the flattening of hierarchies, the ensuing breakdown of organizational boundaries, and the unpredictability of careers, institutions remain what Max Weber calls "imperatively coordinated associations," where respect for authority is crucial for building and maintaining structure. However, we know that, increasingly, employees are skeptical of purely hierarchical power—of fancy job titles and traditional sources of legitimacy such as age and seniority. And they are becoming more suspicious of charisma, as many charismatic leaders turn out to have feet of clay.

What workers need is a sense of moral authority, derived not from a focus on the efficiency of means but from the importance of the ends they produce. The organization of your dreams gives you powerful reasons to submit to its necessary structures that support the organization's purpose. In that company, leaders' authority derives from the answer to a question that Steve Varley, managing partner of Ernst & Young UK, put to senior partners in his inaugural address, after he reported record profits and partners' earnings: "Is that all there is?" (In reply, he proposed a radical new direction—a program called "Growing Successfully, Making the Difference"—aimed at achieving both financial growth and social change.) During the past 30 years we have heard the following kinds of conversations at many organizations: "I'll be home late. I'm working on a cure for migraine." "Still at work. The new U2 album comes out tomorrow—it's brilliant." "Very busy on the plan to take insulin into East Africa." We have never heard this: "I'll be home late. I'm increasing shareholder value."

People want to do good work—to feel they matter in an organization that makes a difference. They want to work in a place that magnifies their strengths, not their weaknesses. For that, they need some autonomy and structure, and the organization must be coherent, honest, and open.

But that's tricky because it requires balancing many competing claims. Achieving the full benefit of diversity means trading the comfort of being surrounded by kindred spirits for the hard work of fitting various kinds of people, work habits, and thought traditions into a vibrant culture. Managers must continually work out when to forge ahead and when to take the time to discuss and compromise.

Our aim here is not to critique modern business structures. But it's hard not to notice that many of the organizations we've highlighted are unusual in their ownership arrangements and ambitions. Featured strongly are partnerships, mutual associations, charitable trusts, and social enterprises. Although all share a desire to generate revenue, few are conventional, large-scale capitalist enterprises.

It would be a mistake to suggest that the organizations are all alike, but two commonalities stand out. First, the institutions are all very clear about what they do well: Novo Nordisk transforms the lives of people with diabetes; Arup creates beautiful environments. Second, the organizations are suspicious, in almost a contrarian way, of fads and fashions that sweep the corporate world.

Work can be liberating, or it can be alienating, exploitative, controlling, and homogenizing. Despite the changes that new technologies and new generations bring, the underlying forces of shareholder capitalism and unexamined bureaucracy remain powerful. As you strive to create an authentic organization and fully realize human potential at work, do not underestimate the challenge. If you do, such organizations will remain the exception rather than the rule—for most people, a mere dream.

Originally published in May 2013. Reprint R1305H

Why Diversity Programs Fail

by Frank Dobbin and Alexandra Kalev

BUSINESSES STARTED CARING A LOT more about diversity after a series of high-profile lawsuits rocked the financial industry. In the late 1990s and early 2000s, Morgan Stanley shelled out $54 million—and Smith Barney and Merrill Lynch more than $100 million each—to settle sex discrimination claims. In 2007, Morgan was back at the table, facing a new class action, which cost the company $46 million. In 2013, Bank of America Merrill Lynch settled a race discrimination suit for $160 million. Cases like these brought Merrill's total 15-year payout to nearly *half a billion* dollars.

It's no wonder that Wall Street firms now require new hires to sign arbitration contracts agreeing not to join class actions. They have also expanded training and other diversity programs. But on balance, equality isn't improving in financial services or elsewhere. Although the proportion of managers at U.S. commercial banks who were Hispanic rose from 4.7% in 2003 to 5.7% in 2014, white women's representation dropped from 39% to 35%, and black men's from 2.5% to 2.3%. The numbers were even worse in investment banks (though that industry is shrinking, which complicates the analysis). Among all U.S. companies with 100 or more employees, the proportion of black men in management increased just slightly—from 3% to 3.3%—from 1985 to 2014. White women saw bigger gains from 1985 to 2000—rising from 22% to 29% of managers—but their numbers haven't budged since then. Even in Silicon Valley, where many leaders tout the need to increase diversity for both business and social justice reasons, bread-and-butter tech jobs remain dominated by white men.

It shouldn't be surprising that most diversity programs aren't increasing diversity. Despite a few new bells and whistles, courtesy of big data, companies are basically doubling down on the same approaches they've used since the 1960s—which often make things worse, not better. Firms have long relied on diversity training to reduce bias on the job, hiring tests and performance ratings to limit it in recruitment and promotions, and grievance systems to give employees a way to challenge managers. Those tools are designed to preempt lawsuits by policing managers' thoughts and actions. Yet laboratory studies show that this kind of force-feeding can activate bias rather than stamp it out. As social scientists have found, people often rebel against rules to assert their autonomy. Try to coerce me to do X, Y, or Z, and I'll do the opposite just to prove that I'm my own person.

In analyzing three decades' worth of data from more than 800 U.S. firms and interviewing hundreds of line managers and executives at length, we've seen that companies get better results when they ease up on the control tactics. It's more effective to engage managers in solving the problem, increase their on-the-job contact with female and minority workers, and promote social accountability—the desire to look fair-minded. That's why interventions such as targeted college recruitment, mentoring programs, self-managed teams, and task forces have boosted diversity in businesses. Some of the most effective solutions aren't even designed with diversity in mind.

Here, we dig into the data, the interviews, and company examples to shed light on what doesn't work and what does.

Why You Can't Just Outlaw Bias

Executives favor a classic command-and-control approach to diversity because it boils expected behaviors down to dos and don'ts that are easy to understand and defend. Yet this approach also flies in the face of nearly everything we know about how to motivate people to

Idea in Brief

The Problem

To reduce bias and increase diversity, organizations are relying on the same programs they've been using since the 1960s. Some of these efforts make matters worse, not better.

The Reason

Most diversity programs focus on controlling managers' behavior, and as studies show, that approach tends to activate bias rather than quash it. People rebel against rules that threaten their autonomy.

The Solution

Instead of trying to police managers' decisions, the most effective programs engage people in working for diversity, increase their contact with women and minorities, and tap into their desire to look good to others.

make changes. Decades of social science research point to a simple truth: You won't get managers on board by blaming and shaming them with rules and reeducation. Let's look at how the most common top-down efforts typically go wrong.

Diversity training

Do people who undergo training usually shed their biases? Researchers have been examining that question since before World War II, in nearly a thousand studies. It turns out that while people are easily taught to respond correctly to a questionnaire about bias, they soon forget the right answers. The positive effects of diversity training rarely last beyond a day or two, and a number of studies suggest that it can activate bias or spark a backlash. Nonetheless, nearly half of midsize companies use it, as do nearly all the *Fortune* 500.

Many firms see adverse effects. One reason is that three-quarters use negative messages in their training. By headlining the legal case for diversity and trotting out stories of huge settlements, they issue an implied threat: "Discriminate, and the company will pay the price." We understand the temptation—that's how we got your attention in the first paragraph—but threats, or "negative incentives," don't win converts.

Another reason is that about three-quarters of firms with training still follow the dated advice of the late diversity guru R. Roosevelt

Thomas Jr. "If diversity management is strategic to the organization," he used to say, diversity training must be mandatory, and management has to make it clear that "if you can't deal with that, then we have to ask you to leave." But five years after instituting required training for managers, companies saw no improvement in the proportion of white women, black men, and Hispanics in management, and the share of black women actually decreased by 9%, on average, while the ranks of Asian-American men and women shrank by 4% to 5%. Trainers tell us that people often respond to compulsory courses with anger and resistance—and many participants actually report more animosity toward other groups afterward.

But voluntary training evokes the opposite response ("I chose to show up, so I must be pro-diversity"), leading to better results: increases of 9% to 13% in black men, Hispanic men, and Asian-American men and women in management five years out (with no decline in white or black women). Research from the University of Toronto reinforces our findings: In one study white subjects read a brochure critiquing prejudice toward blacks. When people felt pressure to agree with it, the reading strengthened their bias against blacks. When they felt the choice was theirs, the reading reduced bias.

Companies too often signal that training is remedial. The diversity manager at a national beverage company told us that the top brass uses it to deal with problem groups. "If there are a number of complaints . . . or, God forbid, some type of harassment case . . . leaders say, 'Everyone in the business unit will go through it again.'" Most companies with training have special programs for managers. To be sure, they're a high-risk group because they make the hiring, promotion, and pay decisions. But singling them out implies that they're the worst culprits. Managers tend to resent that implication and resist the message.

Hiring tests

Some 40% of companies now try to fight bias with mandatory hiring tests assessing the skills of candidates for frontline jobs. But managers don't like being told that they can't hire whomever they please, and our research suggests that they often use the tests selectively. Back in the 1950s, following the postwar migration of blacks northward, Swift & Company, Chicago meatpackers, instituted tests for supervisor and quality-checking jobs. One study found managers telling blacks that they had failed the test and then promoting whites who hadn't been tested. A black machine operator reported: "I had four years at Englewood High School. I took an exam for a checker's job. The foreman told me I failed" and gave the job to a white man who "didn't take the exam."

This kind of thing still happens. When we interviewed the new HR director at a West Coast food company, he said he found that white managers were making only strangers—most of them minorities—take supervisor tests and hiring white friends without testing them. "If you are going to test one person for this particular job title," he told us, "you need to test everybody."

But even managers who test everyone applying for a position may ignore the results. Investment banks and consulting firms build tests into their job interviews, asking people to solve math and scenario-based problems on the spot. While studying this practice, Kellogg professor Lauren Rivera played a fly on the wall during hiring meetings at one firm. She found that the team paid little attention when white men blew the math test but close attention when women and blacks did. Because decision makers (deliberately or not) cherry-picked results, the testing amplified bias rather than quashed it.

Companies that institute written job tests for managers—about 10% have them today—see decreases of 4% to 10% in the share of managerial jobs held by white women, African-American men and women, Hispanic men and women, and Asian-American women over the next five years. There are significant declines among white and Asian-American women—groups with high levels of education, which typically score well on standard managerial tests. So group differences in test-taking skills don't explain the pattern.

Performance ratings

More than 90% of midsize and large companies use annual performance ratings to ensure that managers make fair pay and promotion decisions. Identifying and rewarding the best workers isn't the only goal—the ratings also provide a litigation shield. Companies sued for discrimination often claim that their performance rating systems prevent biased treatment.

But studies show that raters tend to lowball women and minorities in performance reviews. And some managers give everyone high marks to avoid hassles with employees or to keep their options open when handing out promotions. However managers work around performance systems, the bottom line is that ratings don't boost diversity. When companies introduce them, there's no effect on minority managers over the next five years, and the share of white women in management drops by 4%, on average.

Grievance procedures

This last tactic is meant to identify and rehabilitate biased managers. About half of midsize and large firms have systems through which employees can challenge pay, promotion, and termination decisions. But many managers—rather than change their own behavior or address discrimination by others—try to get even with or belittle employees who complain. Among the nearly 90,000 discrimination complaints made to the Equal Employment Opportunity Commission in 2015, 45% included a charge of retaliation—which suggests that the original report was met with ridicule, demotion, or worse.

Once people see that a grievance system isn't warding off bad behavior in their organization, they may become less likely to speak up. Indeed, employee surveys show that most people don't report discrimination. This leads to another unintended consequence: Managers who receive few complaints conclude that their firms don't have a problem. We see this a lot in our interviews. When we talked with the vice president of HR at an electronics firm, she mentioned the widely publicized "difficulties other corporations are having" and added, "We have not had any of those problems . . . we have gone almost four years without any kind of discrimination complaint!" What's more, lab studies show that protective measures like grievance systems lead people to drop their guard and let bias affect their decisions, because they think company policies will guarantee fairness.

Things don't get better when firms put in formal grievance systems; they get worse. Our quantitative analyses show that the managerial ranks of white women and all minority groups except Hispanic men decline—by 3% to 11%—in the five years after companies adopt them.

Still, most employers feel they need some sort of system to intercept complaints, if only because judges like them. One strategy that is gaining ground is the "flexible" complaint system, which offers not only a formal hearing process but also informal mediation. Since an informal resolution doesn't involve hauling the manager before a disciplinary body, it may reduce retaliation. As we'll show, making managers feel accountable without subjecting them to public rebuke tends to help.

Tools for Getting Managers on Board

If these popular solutions backfire, then what can employers do instead to promote diversity?

A number of companies have gotten consistently positive results with tactics that don't focus on control. They apply three basic principles: engage managers in solving the problem, expose them to people from different groups, and encourage social accountability for change.

Engagement

When someone's beliefs and behavior are out of sync, that person experiences what psychologists call "cognitive dissonance." Experiments show that people have a strong tendency to "correct" dissonance by changing either the beliefs or the behavior. So, if you prompt them to act in ways that support a particular view, their opinions shift toward that view. Ask them to write an essay defending the death penalty, and even the penalty's staunch opponents will come to see some merits. When managers actively help boost diversity in their companies, something similar happens: They begin to think of themselves as diversity champions.

Take *college recruitment programs* targeting women and minorities. Our interviews suggest that managers willingly participate when invited. That's partly because the message is positive: "Help us find a greater variety of promising employees!" And involvement is voluntary: Executives sometimes single out managers they think would be good recruiters, but they don't drag anyone along at gunpoint.

Managers who make college visits say they take their charge seriously. They are determined to come back with strong candidates from underrepresented groups—female engineers, for instance, or African-American management trainees. Cognitive dissonance soon kicks in—and managers who were wishy-washy about diversity become converts.

The effects are striking. Five years after a company implements a college recruitment program targeting female employees, the share of white women, black women, Hispanic women, and Asian-American women in its management rises by about 10%, on average. A program focused on minority recruitment increases the proportion of black male managers by 8% and black female managers by 9%.

Mentoring is another way to engage managers and chip away at their biases. In teaching their protégés the ropes and sponsoring them for key training and assignments, mentors help give their charges the breaks they need to develop and advance. The mentors then come to believe that their protégés merit these opportunities—whether they're white men, women, or minorities. That is cognitive dissonance—"Anyone I sponsor must be deserving"—at work again.

While white men tend to find mentors on their own, women and minorities more often need help from formal programs. One reason, as Georgetown's business school dean David Thomas discovered in his research on mentoring, is that white male executives don't feel comfortable reaching out informally to young women and minority men. Yet they are eager to mentor assigned protégés, and women and minorities are often first to sign up for mentors.

Mentoring programs make companies' managerial echelons significantly more diverse: On average they boost the representation of black, Hispanic, and Asian-American women, and Hispanic and Asian-American men, by 9% to 24%. In industries where plenty of college-educated nonmanagers are eligible to move up, like chemicals and electronics, mentoring programs also increase the ranks of white women and black men by 10% or more.

Only about 15% of firms have special college recruitment programs for women and minorities, and only 10% have mentoring programs. Once organizations try them out, though, the upside becomes clear. Consider how these programs helped Coca-Cola in the wake of a race discrimination suit settled in 2000 for a record $193 million. With guidance from a court-appointed external task force, executives in the North America group got involved in recruitment and mentoring initiatives for professionals and middle managers, working specifically toward measurable goals for minorities. Even top leaders helped to recruit and mentor, and talent-sourcing partners were required to broaden their recruitment efforts. After five years, according to former CEO and chairman Neville Isdell, 80% of all mentees had climbed at least one rung in management. Both individual and group mentoring were open to all races but attracted large numbers of African-Americans (who accounted for 36% of protégés). These changes brought important gains. From 2000 to 2006, African-Americans' representation among salaried employees grew from 19.7% to 23%, and Hispanics' from 5.5% to 6.4%. And while African-Americans and Hispanics respectively made up 12% and 4.9% of professionals and middle managers in 2002, just four years later those figures had risen to 15.5% and 5.9%.

This began a virtuous cycle. Today, Coke looks like a different company. This February, *Atlanta Tribune* magazine profiled 17 African-American women in VP roles and above at Coke, including CFO Kathy Waller.

Contact

Evidence that contact between groups can lessen bias first came to light in an unplanned experiment on the European front during World War II. The U.S. army was still segregated, and only whites served in combat roles. High casualties left General Dwight Eisenhower understaffed, and he asked for black volunteers for combat duty. When Harvard sociologist Samuel Stouffer, on leave at the War Department, surveyed troops on their racial attitudes, he found that whites whose companies had been joined by black platoons showed dramatically lower racial animus and greater willingness to work alongside blacks than those whose companies remained segregated.

Stouffer concluded that whites fighting alongside blacks came to see them as soldiers like themselves first and foremost. The key, for Stouffer, was that whites and blacks had to be working toward a common goal *as equals*—hundreds of years of close contact during and after slavery hadn't dampened bias.

Business practices that generate this kind of contact across groups yield similar results. Take *self-managed teams,* which allow people in different roles and functions to work together on projects as equals. Such teams increase contact among diverse types of people, because specialties within firms are still largely divided along racial, ethnic, and gender lines. For example, women are more likely than men to work in sales, whereas white men are more likely to be in tech jobs and management, and black and Hispanic men are more likely to be in production.

As in Stouffer's combat study, working side-by-side breaks down stereotypes, which leads to more equitable hiring and promotion. At firms that create self-managed work teams, the share of white women, black men and women, and Asian-American women in management rises by 3% to 6% over five years.

Rotating management trainees through departments is another way to increase contact. Typically, this kind of *cross-training* allows people to try their hand at various jobs and deepen their understanding of the whole organization. But it also has a positive impact on diversity, because it exposes both department heads and trainees to a wider variety of people. The result, we've seen, is a bump of 3% to 7% in white women, black men and women, and Asian-American men and women in management.

About a third of U.S. firms have self-managed teams for core operations, and nearly four-fifths use cross-training, so these tools are already available in many organizations. Though college recruitment and mentoring have a bigger impact on diversity—perhaps because they activate engagement in the diversity mission *and* create intergroup contact—every bit helps. Self-managed teams and cross-training have had more positive effects than mandatory diversity training, performance evaluations, job testing, or grievance procedures, which are supposed to promote diversity.

Social accountability

The third tactic, encouraging social accountability, plays on our need to look good in the eyes of those around us. It is nicely illustrated by an experiment conducted in Israel. Teachers in training graded identical compositions attributed to Jewish students with Ashkenazic names (European heritage) or with Sephardic names (African or Asian heritage). Sephardic students typically come from poorer families and do worse in school. On average, the teacher trainees gave the Ashkenazic essays Bs and the Sephardic essays Ds. The difference evaporated, however, when trainees were told that they would discuss their grades with peers. The idea that they might have to explain their decisions led them to judge the work by its quality.

In the workplace you'll see a similar effect. Consider this field study conducted by Emilio Castilla of MIT's Sloan School of Management: A firm found it consistently gave African-Americans smaller raises than whites, even when they had identical job titles and performance ratings. So Castilla suggested transparency to activate social accountability. The firm posted each unit's average performance rating and pay raise by race and gender. Once managers realized that employees, peers, and superiors would know which parts of the company favored whites, the gap in raises all but disappeared.

Corporate *diversity task forces* help promote social accountability. CEOs usually assemble these teams, inviting department heads to volunteer and including members of underrepresented groups. Every quarter or two, task forces look at diversity numbers for the whole company, for business units, and for departments to figure out what needs attention.

After investigating where the problems are—recruitment, career bottlenecks, and so on—task force members come up with solutions, which they then take back to their departments. They notice if their colleagues aren't volunteering to mentor or showing up at recruitment events. Accountability theory suggests that having a task force member in a department will cause managers in it to ask themselves, "Will this look right?" when making hiring and promotion decisions.

Which Diversity Efforts Actually Succeed?

IN 829 MIDSIZE AND LARGE U.S. FIRMS, we analyzed how various diversity initiatives affected the proportion of women and minorities in management. Here you can see which ones helped different groups gain ground—and which set them back, despite good intentions. (No bar means we can't say with statistical certainty if the program had any effect.)

Legend:
- ▦ White men
- ▥ White women
- ■ Black men
- ▨ Black women (dark hatched)
- ▧ Hispanic men
- ▨ Hispanic women
- ■ Asian men
- ▩ Asian women

Poor returns on the usual programs

The three most popular interventions made firms less diverse, not more, because managers resisted strong-arming.

% Change over five years

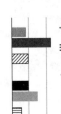

Mandatory diversity training for managers led to significant decreases for Asian-Americans and black women.

Testing job applicants hurts women and minorities—but not because they perform poorly. Hiring managers don't always test everyone (white men often get a pass) and don't interpret results consistently.

Grievance systems likewise reduce diversity pretty much across the board. Though they're meant to re-form biased managers, they often lead to retaliation.

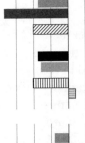

Programs that get results

Companies do a better job of increasing diversity when they forgo the control tactics and frame their efforts more positively. The most effective programs spark engagement, increase contact among different groups, or draw on people's strong desire

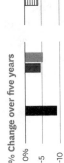

Voluntary training doesn't get managers' defenses up the way mandatory training does—and results in increases for several groups.

Self-managed teams aren't designed to improve diversity, but they help by increasing contact between groups, which are often concentrated in certain functions.

Cross-training also increases managers' exposure to people from different groups. Gains for some groups appear to come at a cost to Hispanic men.

College recruitment targeting women turns recruiting managers into diversity champions, so it also helps boost the numbers for black and Asian-American men.

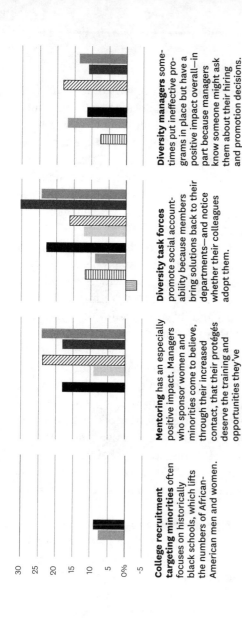

College recruitment targeting minorities often focuses on historically black schools, which lifts the numbers of African-American men and women.

Mentoring has an especially positive impact. Managers who sponsor women and minorities come to believe, through their increased contact, that their protégés deserve the training and opportunities they've received.

Diversity task forces promote social accountability because members bring solutions back to their departments—and notice whether their colleagues adopt them.

Diversity managers sometimes put ineffective programs in place but have a positive impact overall—in part because managers know someone might ask them about their hiring and promotion decisions.

Note: In our analysis, we've isolated the effects of diversity programs from everything else going on in the companies and in the economy.

Deloitte has seen how powerful social accountability can be. In 1992, Mike Cook, who was then the CEO, decided to try to stanch the hemorrhaging of female associates. Half the company's hires were women, but nearly all of them left before they were anywhere near making partner. As Douglas McCracken, CEO of Deloitte's consulting unit at the time, later recounted in HBR, Cook assembled a high-profile task force that "didn't immediately launch a slew of new organizational policies aimed at outlawing bad behavior" but, rather, relied on transparency to get results.

The task force got each office to monitor the career progress of its women and set its own goals to address local problems. When it became clear that the CEO and other managing partners were closely watching, McCracken wrote, "women started getting their share of premier client assignments and informal mentoring." And unit heads all over the country began getting questions from partners and associates about why things weren't changing faster. An external advisory council issued annual progress reports, and individual managers chose change metrics to add to their own performance ratings. In eight years turnover among women dropped to the same level as turnover among men, and the proportion of female partners increased from 5% to 14%—the highest percentage among the big accounting firms. By 2015, 21% of Deloitte's global partners were women, and in March of that year, Deloitte LLP appointed Cathy Engelbert as its CEO—making her the first woman to head a major accountancy.

Task forces are the trifecta of diversity programs. In addition to promoting accountability, they engage members who might have previously been cool to diversity projects and increase contact among the women, minorities, and white men who participate. They pay off, too: On average, companies that put in diversity task forces see 9% to 30% increases in the representation of white women and of each minority group in management over the next five years.

Diversity managers, too, boost inclusion by creating social accountability. To see why, let's go back to the finding of the teacher-in-training experiment, which is supported by many studies: When people know they *might* have to explain their decisions, they are less likely to act on bias. So simply having a diversity manager who could ask them questions prompts managers to step back and consider everyone who is qualified instead of hiring or promoting the first people who come to mind. Companies that appoint diversity managers see 7% to 18% increases in all underrepresented groups— except Hispanic men—in management in the following five years. Those are the gains after accounting for both effective and ineffective programs they put in place.

Only 20% of medium and large employers have task forces, and just 10% have diversity managers, despite the benefits of both. Diversity managers cost money, but task forces use existing workers, so they're a lot cheaper than some of the things that fail, such as mandatory training.

Leading companies like Bank of America Merrill Lynch, Facebook, and Google have placed big bets on accountability in the past couple of years. Expanding on Deloitte's early example, they're now posting complete diversity numbers for all to see. We should know in a few years if that moves the needle for them.

––––––––

Strategies for controlling bias—which drive most diversity efforts— have failed spectacularly since they were introduced to promote equal opportunity. Black men have barely gained ground in corporate management since 1985. White women haven't progressed since 2000. It isn't that there aren't enough educated women and minorities out there—both groups have made huge educational gains over the past two generations. The problem is that we can't motivate people by forcing them to get with the program and punishing them if they don't.

The numbers sum it up. Your organization will become less diverse, not more, if you require managers to go to diversity training, try to regulate their hiring and promotion decisions, and put in a legalistic grievance system.

The very good news is that we know what does work—we just need to do more of it.

Originally published in July–August 2016. Reprint R1607C

When No One Retires

by Paul Irving

BEFORE OUR EYES, THE WORLD is undergoing a massive demographic transformation. In many countries, the population is getting old. Very old. Globally, the number of people age 60 and over is projected to double to more than 2 billion by 2050 and those 60 and over will outnumber children under the age of 5. In the United States, about 10,000 people turn 65 each day, and one in five Americans will be 65 or older by 2030. By 2035, Americans of retirement age will eclipse the number of people aged 18 and under for the first time in U.S. history.

The reasons for this age shift are many—medical advances that keep people healthier longer, dropping fertility rates, and so on—but the net result is the same: Populations around the world will look very different in the decades ahead.

Some in the public and private sector are already taking note—and sounding the alarm. In his first term as chairman of the U.S. Federal Reserve, with the Great Recession looming, Ben Bernanke remarked, "In the coming decades, many forces will shape our economy and our society, but in all likelihood no single factor will have as pervasive an effect as the aging of our population." Back in 2010, Standard & Poor's predicted that the biggest influence on "the future of national economic health, public finances, and policymaking" will be "the irreversible rate at which the world's population is aging."

The world is getting older

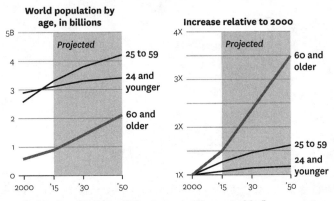

World population by age, in billions

Projected

5B
4
3
2
1
0

2000   '15   '30   '50

25 to 59

24 and younger

60 and older

Increase relative to 2000

Projected

4X
3X
2X
1X

2000   '15   '30   '50

60 and older

25 to 59

24 and younger

Source: United Nations, "World Population Prospects: The 2015 Revision"

This societal shift will undoubtedly change work, too: More and more Americans want to work longer—or have to, given that many aren't saving adequately for retirement. Soon, the workforce will include people from as many as five generations ranging in age from teenagers to 80-somethings.

Are companies prepared? The short answer is "no." Aging will affect every aspect of business operations—whether it's talent recruitment, the structure of compensation and benefits, the development of products and services, how innovation is unlocked, how offices and factories are designed, and even how work is structured—but for some reason, the message just hasn't gotten through. In general, corporate leaders have yet to invest the time and resources necessary to fully grasp the unprecedented ways that aging will change the rules of the game.

What's more, those who *do* think about the impacts of an aging population typically see a looming crisis—not an opportunity. They fail to appreciate the potential that older adults present as workers and consumers. The reality, however, is that increasing longevity contributes to global economic growth. Today's older adults

Idea in Brief

Before our eyes, the world is undergoing a massive demographic transformation. In many countries, the population is aging rapidly. In the United States, about 10,000 people turn 65 each day, and one in five Americans will be 65 or older by 2030. This societal shift will affect every aspect of business operations, but corporate leaders have not yet grasped the unprecedented ways that an aging workforce will change the rules of the game. Those who *do* think about the impacts typically see a looming crisis—not an opportunity. This article helps companies develop a "longevity strategy" for fostering a vibrant multigenerational workforce.

are generally healthier and more active than those of generations past, and they are changing the nature of retirement as they continue to learn, work, and contribute. In the workplace, they provide emotional stability, complex problem-solving skills, nuanced thinking, and institutional know-how. Their talents complement those of younger workers, and their guidance and support enhance performance and intergenerational collaboration. In encore careers, volunteering, and civic and social settings, their experience and problem-solving abilities contribute to society's well-being.

In the public sector, policy makers are beginning to take action. Efforts are under way in the United States to reimagine communities to enhance "age friendliness," develop strategies to improve infrastructure, enhance wellness and disease prevention, and design new ways to invest for retirement as traditional income sources like pensions and defined benefit plans dry up. But such efforts are still early stage, and given the slow pace of governmental change they will likely take years to evolve.

Companies, by contrast, are uniquely positioned to change practices and attitudes *now*. Transformation won't be easy, but companies that move past today's preconceptions about older employees and respond and adapt to changing demographics will realize significant dividends, generating new possibilities for financial return and enhancing the lives of their employees and customers. I spent many years in executive management, corporate law, and board service.

Based on this experience, along with research conducted with Arielle Burstein, Kevin Proff, and other members of our staff at the Milken Institute Center for the Future of Aging, I have developed a framework for building a "longevity strategy" that companies can use to create a vibrant multigenerational workforce. Broadly, a longevity strategy should include two key elements: internal-facing activities (hiring, retention, and mining the talents of workers of all ages) and external-facing ones (how your company positions itself and its products and services to customers and stakeholders). In this article, I'll address the internal activities companies should be engaging in.

But first, let's examine why leaders seem to be overlooking the opportunities of an aging population.

The Ageism Effect

There's broad consensus that the global population is changing and growing significantly older. There's also a prevailing opinion that the impacts on society will largely be negative. A Government Accountability Office report warns that older populations will bring slower growth, lower productivity, and increasing dependency on society. A report from the Congressional Budget Office projects that higher entitlement costs associated with an aging population will drive up expenses relative to revenues, increasing the federal deficit. The World Bank foresees fading potential in economies across the globe, warning in 2018 of "headwinds from ageing populations in both advanced and developing economies, expecting decreased labour supply and productivity growth." Such predictions serve to further entrench the belief that older workers are an expensive drag on society.

What's at the heart of this gloomy outlook? Economists often refer to what's known as the dependency ratio: the number of people not typically in the workforce—those younger than 15 and older than 65—in a population divided by the number of working-age people. This measure assumes that older adults are generally unproductive and can be expected to do little other than consume benefits in their later years. Serious concerns about the so-called "silver tsunami" are justified if this assumption is correct: The prospect of a massive

The global aging phenomenon

Projected breakdown of world population, by region

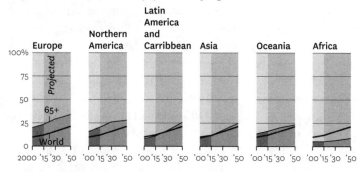

Note: Northern America consists of Canada and the United States.
Source: United Nations, "World Population Prospects: The 2015 Revision"

population of sick, disengaged, lonely, needy, and cognitively impaired people is a dark one indeed.

This picture, however, is simply not accurate. While some older adults do suffer from disabling physical and cognitive conditions or are otherwise unable to maintain an active lifestyle, far more are able and inclined to stay in the game longer, disproving assumptions about their prospects for work and productivity. The work of Laura Carstensen and her colleagues at the Stanford Center on Longevity shows that typical 60-something workers today are healthy, experienced, and more likely than younger colleagues to be satisfied with their jobs. They have a strong work ethic and loyalty to their employers. They are motivated, knowledgeable, adept at resolving social dilemmas, and care more about meaningful contributions and less about self-advancement. They are more likely than their younger counterparts to build social cohesion and to share information and organizational values.

Yet the flawed perceptions persist, a byproduct of stubborn and pervasive ageism. Positive attributes of older workers are crowded out by negative stereotypes that infect work settings and devalue older adults in a youth-oriented culture. Older adults regularly find themselves on the losing end of hiring decisions, promotions, and even volunteer opportunities. Research from AARP found that approximately two-thirds of workers ages 45 to 74 said they have seen or experienced age discrimination in the workplace. Of those, a remarkable 92% said age discrimination is very, or somewhat, common. Research for the Federal Reserve Bank of San Francisco backs this up. A study involving 40,000 made-up résumés found compelling evidence that older applicants, especially women, suffer consistent age discrimination. A case in point is IBM, which is currently facing allegations of using improper practices to marginalize and terminate older workers.

There's more: Deloitte's 2018 Global Human Capital Trends study found that 20% of business and HR leaders surveyed viewed older workers as a competitive disadvantage and an impediment to the progress of younger workers. The report concludes that "there may be a significant hidden problem of age bias in the workforce today." It also warns that "left unaddressed, perceptions that a company's culture and employment practices suffer from age bias could damage its brand and social capital."

The negative cultural overlay about aging is reinforced by media and advertising that often portray older adults in clichéd, patronizing ways. A classic example is Life Alert's ad from the 1980s for its medical alert necklace, immortalizing the phrase "I've fallen, and I can't get up!" Recent ads by E*TRADE and Postmates have also drawn criticism as ageist. A more subtle, but just as damaging example is the trumpeting of "anti-aging" benefits on beauty products as a marketing tool, suggesting that growing older is, by definition, a negative process.

Some companies are pushing back: In a recent video, T-Mobile's John Legere took on the topic of ageist stereotypes while promoting a T-Mobile service for adults age 55-plus. He chided competitors for what he called their belittling treatment of older adults in marketing campaigns that emphasize large-size phone buttons and imply that boomers are tech idiots. "Degrading at the highest level," Legere calls it. "The carriers assume boomers are a bunch of old people stuck in the past who can't figure out how the internet works. News flash, carriers: Boomers invented the internet."

Yet for the most part, employers continue to invest far more in young employees and generally do not train workers over 50. In fact, many companies would rather not think about the existence of older workers all. "Today it is socially unacceptable to ignore, ridicule, or stereotype someone based on their gender, race, or sexual orientation," points out Jo Ann Jenkins, the CEO of AARP. "So why is it still acceptable to do this to people based on their age?"

Over the past decades, companies have recognized the economic and social benefits of women, people of color, and LGBT individuals in the workforce. These priority initiatives must be continued—obviously, we're not even close to achieving genuine equality in the corporate world; at the same time, the inclusion of older adults in the business diversity matrix is long overdue. Patricia Milligan, senior partner and global leader for Mercer's Multinational Client Group, observes, "At the most respected multinational companies, the single class not represented from a diversity and inclusion perspective is older workers. LGBT, racial and ethnic diversity, women, people with physical disabilities, veterans—you can find an affinity group in a corporation for everything, except an older worker."

The U.S. labor force is getting older, too

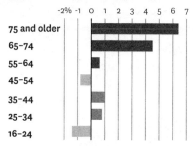

Projected average annual growth rate by age group, 2014 to 2024

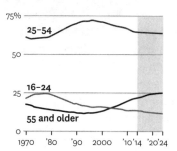

Breakdown by age group, 1970 to 2024

Source: U.S. Bureau of Labor Statistics

151

Managing a Multigenerational Workforce

How can companies push past stereotypes and other organizational impediments to tap into a thriving and talented population of older workers? A range of best practices have been emerging, and some companies are making real progress. Each points to specific changes companies should be considering as they develop their own strategies.

Redefine the workweek

To start, you need to reconsider the out-of-date idea that all employees work Monday through Friday, from 9 to 5, in the same office. The notion that everyone retires completely by age 65 should also be jettisoned. Companies instead should invest in opportunities for creative mentorship, part-time work, flex-hour schedules, and sabbatical programs geared to the abilities and inclinations of older workers. Programs that offer preretirement and career transition support, coaching, counseling, and encore career pathways can also make employees more engaged and productive. Many older workers say they are ready to exchange high salaries for flexible schedules and phased retirements. Some companies have already embraced nontraditional work programs for employees, creating a new kind of environment for success. The CVS "Snowbird" program, for example, allows older employees to travel and work seasonally in different CVS pharmacy regions. Home Depot recruits and hires thousands of retired construction workers, making the most of their expertise on the sales floor. The National Institutes of Health, half of whose workforce is over 50, actively recruits at 50-plus job fairs and offers benefits such as flexible schedules, telecommuting, and exercise classes. Steelcase offers workers a phased retirement program with reduced hours. Michelin has rehired retirees to oversee projects, foster community relations, and facilitate employee mentoring. Brooks Brothers consults with older workers on equipment and process design, and restructures assignments to offer enhanced flexibility for its aging workforce.

Reimagine the workplace

Your company should also be prepared to adjust workspaces to improve ergonomics and make environments more age-friendly for older employees. No one should be distracted from their tasks by pain that can be prevented or eased, and even small changes can improve health, safety, and productivity. Xerox, for example, has an ergonomic training program aimed at reducing musculoskeletal disorders in its aging workforce. BMW and Nissan have implemented changes to their manufacturing lines to accommodate older workers, ranging from barbershop-style chairs and better-designed tools to "cobot" (collaborative robot) partners that manage complicated tasks and lift heavier objects. The good news is that programs that improve the lives of older workers can be equally valuable for younger counterparts.

Mind the mix

Lastly, you need to consider and monitor the age mixes in your departments and teams. Many companies will need to manage as many as five generations of workers in the near future, if they aren't already. Some pernicious biases can make this difficult. For example, research shows that every generation wants meaningful work—but that each believes everyone else is just in it for the money. Companies should emphasize workers' shared value. "Companies pursuing Millennial-specific employee engagement strategies are wasting time, focus, and money," Bruce Pfau, the former vice chair of human resources at KPMG, argues. "They would be far better served to focus on factors that lead all employees to join, stay, and perform at their best."

By tapping ways that workers of different generations can augment and learn from each other, companies set themselves up for success over the long term. Young workers can benefit from the mentorship of older colleagues, and a promising workforce resource lies in intergenerational collaboration, combining the energy and speed of youth with the wisdom and experience of age.

PNC Financial Group uses multigenerational teams to help the company compete more effectively in the financial markets through a better understanding of the target audience for products. Pharma giant Pfizer has experimented with a "senior intern" program to reap the benefits of multigenerational collaboration. In the tech world, Airbnb recruited former hotel mogul Chip Conley to provide experienced management perspective to his younger colleagues. Pairing younger and older workers in all phases of product and service innovation and design can create opportunity for professional growth. And facilitating intergenerational relationships, mentoring, training, and teaming mitigate isolation and help break down walls.

To begin this process, start talking to your employees of all ages. And get them to talk with each other about their goals, interests, needs, and worries. Young and old workers share similar anxieties and hopes about work—and also have differences that need to be better understood companywide. Look for opportunities for engagement between generations and places where older and younger workers can support one another through skill development and mentorship. After all, if everyone needs and wants to work, we're going to have to learn to work together.

To be clear, all of these changes—from flexible hours to team makeup—will require a recalibration of company processes, some of which are deeply ingrained. Leaders must ask, do our current health insurance, sick leave, caregiving, and vacation policies accommodate people who work reduced hours? Do our employee performance-measurement systems appropriately recognize and reward the strengths of older workers? Currently, most companies focus on individual achievement as opposed to team success. This may inadvertently punish older employees who offer other types of value—like mentorship, forging deep relationships with clients and colleagues, and conflict resolution—that are not as easily captured using traditional assessment tools. Here, too, initiatives aimed at older workers can benefit other workers as well. For instance, research suggests that evaluating team performance also tends to boost the careers of employees from low-income backgrounds.

Turning a Crisis into an Opportunity

I'm admittedly bullish about the positive aspects of working longer and believe that company leaders can harness the opportunity of an aging population to gain competitive advantage. But I'm not oblivious to the challenges a longevity strategy poses. We're talking about initiating a massive culture change for firms—a change that must come from the top.

But ignoring the realities of the demographic shift under way is no longer an option. CEOs and senior executives will need to put the issue front and center with HR leaders, product developers, marketing managers, investors, and many other stakeholders who may not have it on their radar screens. This will take guts and persistence: Leaders must bravely say, "We reject the assumption that people become less tech-savvy as they get older" and "We will fight the impulse to put only our youngest employees on new initiatives." To genuinely make headway on this long-range issue, companies will have to make tough, and sometimes unpopular, decisions, especially in a world where short-term results and demands dominate leaders' agendas. But isn't that what great leaders do?

The business community has a chance to spearhead a broad movement to change culture, create opportunity, and drive growth. In doing so, companies will improve not only mature lives, but lives of all ages, and the prospects of workers for generations to come. This transformative movement to realize the potential of the 21st century's changing demography is the next big test for corporate leadership.

Originally published on hbr.org in November 2018. Reprint BG1806

Collaborative Intelligence

Humans and AI Are Joining Forces.
by H. James Wilson and Paul R. Daugherty

ARTIFICIAL INTELLIGENCE IS BECOMING good at many "human" jobs—diagnosing disease, translating languages, providing customer service—and it's improving fast. This is raising reasonable fears that AI will ultimately replace human workers throughout the economy. But that's not the inevitable, or even most likely, outcome. Never before have digital tools been so responsive to us, nor we to our tools. While AI will radically alter how work gets done and who does it, the technology's larger impact will be in complementing and augmenting human capabilities, not replacing them.

Certainly, many companies have used AI to automate processes, but those that deploy it mainly to displace employees will see only short-term productivity gains. In our research involving 1,500 companies, we found that firms achieve the most significant performance improvements when humans and machines work together (see the exhibit "The value of collaboration"). Through such collaborative intelligence, humans and AI actively enhance each other's complementary strengths: the leadership, teamwork, creativity, and social skills of the former, and the speed, scalability, and quantitative capabilities of the latter. What comes naturally to people (making a joke, for example) can be tricky for machines, and

The value of collaboration

Companies benefit from optimizing collaboration between humans and artificial intelligence. Five principles can help them do so: Reimagine business processes; embrace experimentation/employee involvement; actively direct AI strategy; responsibly collect data; and redesign work to incorporate AI and cultivate related employee skills. A survey of 1,075 companies in 12 industries found that the more of these principles companies adopted, the better their AI initiatives performed in terms of speed, cost savings, revenues, or other operational measures.

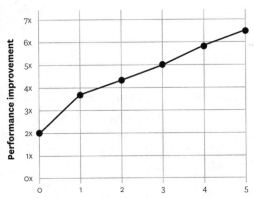

**Number of human-machine collaboration principles adopted
(0 indicates the adoption of only basic, noncollaborative AI)**

what's straightforward for machines (analyzing gigabytes of data) remains virtually impossible for humans. Business requires both kinds of capabilities.

To take full advantage of this collaboration, companies must understand how humans can most effectively augment machines, how machines can enhance what humans do best, and how to redesign business processes to support the partnership. Through our research and work in the field, we have developed guidelines to help companies achieve this and put the power of collaborative intelligence to work.

Idea in Brief

The Outlook

Artificial intelligence is transforming business—and having the most significant impact when it augments human workers instead of replacing them.

The Details

Companies see the biggest performance gains when humans and smart machines collaborate. People are needed to train machines, explain their outputs, and ensure their responsible use. AI,

in turn, can enhance humans' cognitive skills and creativity, free workers from low-level tasks, and extend their physical capabilities.

The Prescription

Companies should reimagine their business processes, focusing on using AI to achieve more operational flexibility or speed, greater scale, better decision making, or increased personalization of products and services.

Humans Assisting Machines

Humans need to perform three crucial roles. They must *train* machines to perform certain tasks; *explain* the outcomes of those tasks, especially when the results are counterintuitive or controversial; and *sustain* the responsible use of machines (by, for example, preventing robots from harming humans).

Training

Machine-learning algorithms must be taught how to perform the work they're designed to do. In that effort, huge training data sets are amassed to teach machine-translation apps to handle idiomatic expressions, medical apps to detect disease, and recommendation engines to support financial decision making. In addition, AI systems must be trained how best to interact with humans. While organizations across sectors are now in the early stages of filling trainer roles, leading tech companies and research groups already have mature training staffs and expertise.

Consider Microsoft's AI assistant, Cortana. The bot required extensive training to develop just the right personality: confident, caring, and helpful but not bossy. Instilling those qualities took countless hours of attention by a team that included a poet, a novelist, and a playwright. Similarly, human trainers were needed to develop the personalities of Apple's Siri and Amazon's Alexa to ensure that they accurately reflected their companies' brands. Siri, for example, has just a touch of sassiness, as consumers might expect from Apple.

AI assistants are now being trained to display even more complex and subtle human traits, such as sympathy. The start-up Koko, an offshoot of the MIT Media Lab, has developed technology that can help AI assistants seem to commiserate. For instance, if a user is having a bad day, the Koko system doesn't reply with a canned response such as "I'm sorry to hear that." Instead it may ask for more information and then offer advice to help the person see his issues in a different light. If he were feeling stressed, for instance, Koko might recommend thinking of that tension as a positive emotion that could be channeled into action.

Explaining

As AIs increasingly reach conclusions through processes that are opaque (the so-called black-box problem), they require human experts in the field to explain their behavior to nonexpert users. These "explainers" are particularly important in evidence-based industries, such as law and medicine, where a practitioner needs to understand how an AI weighed inputs into, say, a sentencing or medical recommendation. Explainers are similarly important in helping insurers and law enforcement understand why an autonomous car took actions that led to an accident—or failed to avoid one. And explainers are becoming integral in regulated industries—indeed, in any consumer-facing industry where a machine's output could be challenged as unfair, illegal, or just plain wrong. For instance, the European Union's new General Data Protection Regulation (GDPR) gives consumers the right to receive an explanation for any algorithm-based decision, such as the rate offer on a credit card or mortgage. This is one area where AI will contribute to *increased* employment: Experts estimate that companies will have to create about 75,000 new jobs to administer the GDPR requirements.

Sustaining

In addition to having people who can explain AI outcomes, companies need "sustainers"—employees who continually work to ensure that AI systems are functioning properly, safely, and responsibly.

For example, an array of experts sometimes referred to as safety engineers focus on anticipating and trying to prevent harm by AIs. The developers of industrial robots that work alongside people have paid careful attention to ensuring that they recognize humans nearby and don't endanger them. These experts may also review analysis from explainers when AIs do cause harm, as when a self-driving car is involved in a fatal accident.

Other groups of sustainers make sure that AI systems uphold ethical norms. If an AI system for credit approval, for example, is found to be discriminating against people in certain groups (as has happened), these ethics managers are responsible for investigating and addressing the problem. Playing a similar role, data compliance officers try to ensure that the data that is feeding AI systems complies with the GDPR and other consumer-protection regulations. A related data-use role involves ensuring that AIs manage information responsibly. Like many tech companies, Apple uses AI to collect personal details about users as they engage with the company's devices and software. The aim is to improve the user experience, but unconstrained data gathering can compromise privacy, anger customers, and run afoul of the law. The company's "differential privacy team" works to make sure that while the AI seeks to learn as much as possible about a group of users in a statistical sense, it is protecting the privacy of individual users.

Machines Assisting Humans

Smart machines are helping humans expand their abilities in three ways. They can *amplify* our cognitive strengths; *interact* with customers and employees to free us for higher-level tasks; and *embody* human skills to extend our physical capabilities.

Enhancing performance

At organizations in all kinds of industries, humans and AI are collaborating to improve five elements of business processes.

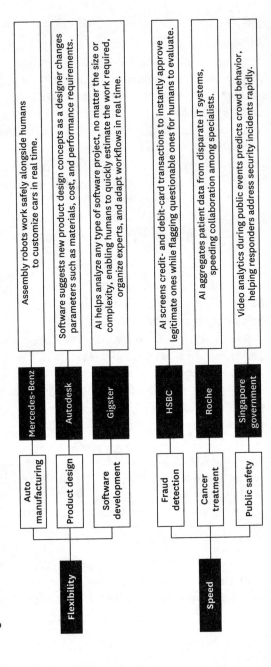

Flexibility

Auto manufacturing	Mercedes-Benz	Assembly robots work safely alongside humans to customize cars in real time.
Product design	Autodesk	Software suggests new product design concepts as a designer changes parameters such as materials, cost, and performance requirements.
Software development	Gigster	AI helps analyze any type of software project, no matter the size or complexity, enabling humans to quickly estimate the work required, organize experts, and adapt workflows in real time.

Speed

Fraud detection	HSBC	AI screens credit- and debit-card transactions to instantly approve legitimate ones while flagging questionable ones for humans to evaluate.
Cancer treatment	Roche	AI aggregates patient data from disparate IT systems, speeding collaboration among specialists.
Public safety	Singapore government	Video analytics during public events predicts crowd behavior, helping responders address security incidents rapidly.

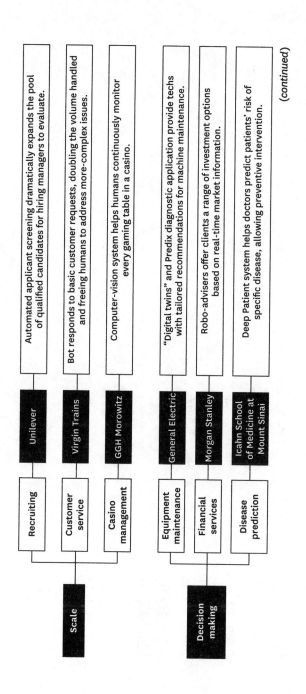

Scale			
Recruiting	Unilever	Automated applicant screening dramatically expands the pool of qualified candidates for hiring managers to evaluate.
Customer service	Virgin Trains	Bot responds to basic customer requests, doubling the volume handled and freeing humans to address more-complex issues.
Casino management	GGH Morowitz	Computer-vision system helps humans continuously monitor every gaming table in a casino.

Decision making			
Equipment maintenance	General Electric	"Digital twins" and Predix diagnostic application provide techs with tailored recommendations for machine maintenance.
Financial services	Morgan Stanley	Robo-advisers offer clients a range of investment options based on real-time market information.
Disease prediction	Icahn School of Medicine at Mount Sinai	Deep Patient system helps doctors predict patients' risk of specific disease, allowing preventive intervention.

(continued)

Enhancing performance (*continued*)

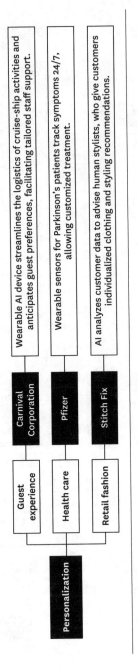

Personalization		
Guest experience	Carnival Corporation	Wearable AI device streamlines the logistics of cruise-ship activities and anticipates guest preferences, facilitating tailored staff support.
Health care	Pfizer	Wearable sensors for Parkinson's patients track symptoms 24/7, allowing customized treatment.
Retail fashion	Stitch Fix	AI analyzes customer data to advise human stylists, who give customers individualized clothing and styling recommendations.

Amplifying

Artificial intelligence can boost our analytic and decision-making abilities by providing the right information at the right time. But it can also heighten creativity. Consider how Autodesk's Dreamcatcher AI enhances the imagination of even exceptional designers. A designer provides Dreamcatcher with criteria about the desired product—for example, a chair able to support up to 300 pounds, with a seat 18 inches off the ground, made of materials costing less than $75, and so on. She can also supply information about other chairs that she finds attractive. Dreamcatcher then churns out thousands of designs that match those criteria, often sparking ideas that the designer might not have initially considered. She can then guide the software, telling it which chairs she likes or doesn't, leading to a new round of designs.

Throughout the iterative process, Dreamcatcher performs the myriad calculations needed to ensure that each proposed design meets the specified criteria. This frees the designer to concentrate on deploying uniquely human strengths: professional judgment and aesthetic sensibilities.

Interacting

Human-machine collaboration enables companies to interact with employees and customers in novel, more effective ways. AI agents like Cortana, for example, can facilitate communications between people or on behalf of people, such as by transcribing a meeting and distributing a voice-searchable version to those who couldn't attend. Such applications are inherently scalable—a single chatbot, for instance, can provide routine customer service to large numbers of people simultaneously, wherever they may be.

SEB, a major Swedish bank, now uses a virtual assistant called Aida to interact with millions of customers. Able to handle natural-language conversations, Aida has access to vast stores of data and can answer many frequently asked questions, such as how to open an account or make cross-border payments. She can also ask callers follow-up questions to solve their problems, and she's able to analyze a caller's tone of voice (frustrated versus appreciative, for instance) and use that information to provide better service later. Whenever the system can't resolve an issue—which happens in about 30% of cases—it turns the caller over to a human customer-service representative and then monitors that interaction to learn how to resolve similar problems in the future. With Aida handling basic requests, human reps can concentrate on addressing more-complex issues, especially those from unhappy callers who might require extra hand-holding.

Embodying

Many AIs, like Aida and Cortana, exist principally as digital entities, but in other applications the intelligence is embodied in a robot that augments a human worker. With their sophisticated sensors, motors, and actuators, AI-enabled machines can now recognize people and objects and work safely alongside humans in factories, warehouses, and laboratories.

In manufacturing, for example, robots are evolving from potentially dangerous and "dumb" industrial machines into smart, context-aware "cobots." A cobot arm might, for example, handle repetitive actions that require heavy lifting, while a person performs complementary tasks that require dexterity and human judgment, such as assembling a gear motor.

Hyundai is extending the cobot concept with exoskeletons. These wearable robotic devices, which adapt to the user and location in real time, will enable industrial workers to perform their jobs with superhuman endurance and strength.

Reimagining Your Business

In order to get the most value from AI, operations need to be redesigned. To do this, companies must first discover and describe an operational area that can be improved. It might be a balky internal process (such as HR's slowness to fill staff positions), or it could be a previously intractable problem that can now be addressed using AI (such as quickly identifying adverse drug reactions across patient

Revealing Invisible Problems

FORMER U.S. DEFENSE SECRETARY Donald Rumsfeld once famously distinguished among "known knowns," "known unknowns," and "unknown unknowns"—things you're not even aware you don't know. Some companies are now using AI to uncover unknown unknowns in their businesses. Case in point: GNS Healthcare applies machine-learning software to find overlooked relationships among data in patients' health records and elsewhere. After identifying a relationship, the software churns out numerous hypotheses to explain it and then suggests which of those are the most likely. This approach enabled GNS to uncover a new drug interaction hidden in unstructured patient notes. CEO Colin Hill points out that this is not garden-variety data mining to find associations. "Our machine-learning platform is not just about seeing patterns and correlations in data," he says. "It's about actually discovering causal links."

populations). Moreover, a number of new AI and advanced analytic techniques can help surface previously invisible problems that are amenable to AI solutions (see the sidebar "Revealing Invisible Problems").

Next, companies must develop a solution through co-creation—having stakeholders envision how they might collaborate with AI systems to improve a process. Consider the case of a large agricultural company that wanted to deploy AI technology to help farmers. An enormous amount of data was available about soil properties, weather patterns, historical harvests, and so forth, and the initial plan was to build an AI application that would more accurately predict future crop yields. But in discussions with farmers, the company learned of a more pressing need. What farmers really wanted was a system that could provide real-time recommendations on how to increase productivity—which crops to plant, where to grow them, how much nitrogen to use in the soil, and so on. The company developed an AI system to provide such advice, and the initial outcomes were promising; farmers were happy about the crop yields obtained with the AI's guidance. Results from that initial test were then fed back into the system to refine the algorithms used. As with the discovery step, new AI and analytic techniques can assist in co-creation by suggesting novel approaches to improving processes.

The third step for companies is to scale and then sustain the proposed solution. SEB, for example, originally deployed a version of Aida internally to assist 15,000 bank employees but thereafter rolled out the chatbot to its one million customers.

Through our work with hundreds of companies, we have identified five characteristics of business processes that companies typically want to improve: flexibility, speed, scale, decision making, and personalization. When reimagining a business process, determine which of these characteristics is central to the desired transformation, how intelligent collaboration could be harnessed to address it, and what alignments and trade-offs with other process characteristics will be necessary.

Flexibility

For Mercedes-Benz executives, inflexible processes presented a growing challenge. Increasingly, the company's most profitable customers had been demanding individualized S-class sedans, but the automaker's assembly systems couldn't deliver the customization people wanted.

Traditionally, car manufacturing has been a rigid process with automated steps executed by "dumb" robots. To improve flexibility, Mercedes replaced some of those robots with AI-enabled cobots and redesigned its processes around human-machine collaborations. At the company's plant near Stuttgart, Germany, cobot arms guided by human workers pick up and place heavy parts, becoming an extension of the worker's body. This system puts the worker in control of the build of each car, doing less manual labor and more of a "piloting" job with the robot.

The company's human-machine teams can adapt on the fly. In the plant, the cobots can be reprogrammed easily with a tablet, allowing them to handle different tasks depending on changes in the workflow. Such agility has enabled the manufacturer to achieve unprecedented levels of customization. Mercedes can individualize vehicle production according to the real-time choices consumers make at dealerships, changing everything from a vehicle's dashboard components to the seat leather to the tire valve caps. As a result, no two cars rolling off the assembly line at the Stuttgart plant are the same.

Speed

For some business activities, the premium is on speed. One such operation is the detection of credit-card fraud. Companies have just seconds to determine whether they should approve a given transaction. If it's fraudulent, they will most likely have to eat that loss. But if they deny a legitimate transaction, they lose the fee from that purchase and anger the customer.

Like most major banks, HSBC has developed an AI-based solution that improves the speed and accuracy of fraud detection. The AI monitors and scores millions of transactions daily, using data on purchase location and customer behavior, IP addresses, and other information to identify subtle patterns that signal possible fraud. HSBC first implemented the system in the United States, significantly reducing the rate of undetected fraud and false positives, and then rolled it out in the UK and Asia. A different AI system used by Danske Bank improved its fraud-detection rate by 50% and decreased false positives by 60%. The reduction in the number of false positives frees investigators to concentrate their efforts on equivocal transactions the AI has flagged, where human judgment is needed.

The fight against financial fraud is like an arms race: Better detection leads to more-devious criminals, which leads to better detection, which continues the cycle. Thus the algorithms and scoring models for combating fraud have a very short shelf life and require continual updating. In addition, different countries and regions use different models. For these reasons, legions of data analysts, IT professionals, and experts in financial fraud are needed at the interface between humans and machines to keep the software a step ahead of the criminals.

Scale

For many business processes, poor scalability is the primary obstacle to improvement. That's particularly true of processes that depend on intensive human labor with minimal machine assistance.

Consider, for instance, the employee recruitment process at Unilever. The consumer goods giant was looking for a way to diversify its 170,000-person workforce. HR determined that it needed to focus on entry-level hires and then fast-track the best into management. But the company's existing processes weren't able to evaluate potential recruits in sufficient numbers—while giving each applicant individual attention—to ensure a diverse population of exceptional talent.

Here's how Unilever combined human and AI capabilities to scale individualized hiring: In the first round of the application process, candidates are asked to play online games that help assess traits such as risk aversion. These games have no right or wrong answers, but they help Unilever's AI figure out which individuals might be best suited for a particular position. In the next round, applicants are asked to submit a video in which they answer questions designed for the specific position they're interested in. Their responses are analyzed by an AI system that considers not just what they say but also their body language and tone. The best candidates from that round, as judged by the AI, are then invited to Unilever for in-person interviews, after which humans make the final hiring decisions.

It's too early to tell whether the new recruiting process has resulted in better employees. The company has been closely tracking the success of those hires, but more data is still needed. It is clear, however, that the new system has greatly broadened the scale of Unilever's recruiting. In part because job seekers can easily access the system by smartphone, the number of applicants doubled to 30,000 within a year, the number of universities represented surged from 840 to 2,600, and the socioeconomic diversity of new hires increased. Furthermore, the average time from application to hiring decision has dropped from four months to just four weeks, while the time that recruiters spend reviewing applications has fallen by 75%.

Decision making
By providing employees with tailored information and guidance, AI can help them reach better decisions. This can be especially valuable for workers in the trenches, where making the right call can have a huge impact on the bottom line.

Consider the way in which equipment maintenance is being improved with the use of "digital twins"—virtual models of physical equipment. General Electric builds such software models of its turbines and other industrial products and continually updates them with operating data streaming from the equipment. By collecting readings from large numbers of machines in the field, GE has amassed a wealth of information on normal and aberrant performance. Its Predix application, which uses machine-learning algorithms, can now predict when a specific part in an individual machine might fail.

This technology has fundamentally changed the decision-intensive process of maintaining industrial equipment. Predix might, for example, identify some unexpected rotor wear and tear in a turbine, check the turbine's operational history, report that the damage has increased fourfold over the past few months, and warn that if nothing is done, the rotor will lose an estimated 70% of its useful life. The system can then suggest appropriate actions, taking into account the machine's current condition, the operating environment, and aggregated data about similar damage and repairs to other machines. Along with its recommendations, Predix can generate information about their costs and financial benefits and provide a confidence level (say, 95%) for the assumptions used in its analysis.

Without Predix, workers would be lucky to catch the rotor damage on a routine maintenance check. It's possible that it would go undetected until the rotor failed, resulting in a costly shutdown. With Predix, maintenance workers are alerted to potential problems before they become serious, and they have the needed information at their fingertips to make good decisions—ones that can sometimes save GE millions of dollars.

Personalization

Providing customers with individually tailored brand experiences is the holy grail of marketing. With AI, such personalization can now be achieved with previously unimaginable precision and at vast scale. Think of the way the music streaming service Pandora uses AI algorithms to generate personalized playlists for each of its millions of users according to their preferences in songs, artists, and genres. Or consider Starbucks, which, with customers' permission, uses AI to recognize their mobile devices and call up their ordering history to help baristas make serving recommendations. The AI technology does what it does best, sifting through and processing copious amounts of data to recommend certain offerings or actions, and humans do what they do best, exercising their intuition and judgment to make a recommendation or select the best fit from a set of choices.

The Carnival Corporation is applying AI to personalize the cruise experience for millions of vacationers through a wearable device called the Ocean Medallion and a network that allows smart devices to connect. Machine learning dynamically processes the data flowing from the medallion and from sensors and systems throughout the ship to help guests get the most out of their vacations. The medallion streamlines the boarding and debarking processes, tracks the guests' activities, simplifies purchasing by connecting their credit cards to the device, and acts as a room key. It also connects to a system that anticipates guests' preferences, helping crew members deliver personalized service to each guest by suggesting tailored itineraries of activities and dining experiences.

The Need for New Roles and Talent

Reimagining a business process involves more than the implementation of AI technology; it also requires a significant commitment to developing employees with what we call "fusion skills"—those that enable them to work effectively at the human-machine interface. To start, people must learn to delegate tasks to the new technology, as when physicians trust computers to help read X-rays and MRIs. Employees should also know how to combine their distinctive human skills with those of a smart machine to get a better outcome than either could achieve alone, as in robot-assisted surgery. Workers must be able to teach intelligent agents new skills and undergo training to work well within AI-enhanced processes. For example, they must know how best to put questions to an AI agent to get the information they need. And there must be employees, like those on Apple's differential privacy team, who ensure that their companies' AI systems are used responsibly and not for illegal or unethical purposes.

We expect that in the future, company roles will be redesigned around the desired outcomes of reimagined processes, and corporations will increasingly be organized around different types of skills rather than around rigid job titles. AT&T has already begun that transition as it shifts from landline telephone services to mobile networks and starts to retrain 100,000 employees for new positions. As part of that effort, the company has completely overhauled its organizational chart: Approximately 2,000 job titles have been streamlined into a much smaller number of broad categories encompassing similar skills. Some of those skills are what one might expect (for example, proficiency in data science and data wrangling), while others are less obvious (for instance, the ability to use simple machine-learning tools to cross-sell services).

Most activities at the human-machine interface require people to *do new and different things* (such as train a chatbot) and to *do things differently* (use that chatbot to provide better customer service). So far, however, only a small number of the companies we've surveyed have begun to reimagine their business processes to optimize collaborative intelligence. But the lesson is clear: Organizations that use machines merely to displace workers through automation will miss the full potential of AI. Such a strategy is misguided from the get-go. Tomorrow's leaders will instead be those that embrace collaborative intelligence, transforming their operations, their markets, their industries, and—no less important—their workforces.

Originally published in July–August 2018. Reprint R1804J

DOMINIC BARTON is the global managing partner of McKinsey & Company. He is a coauthor of *Talent Wins: The New Playbook for Putting People First* (Harvard Business Review Press, 2018).

MARCUS BUCKINGHAM provides performance management tools and training to organizations. He is the author of *StandOut 2.0: Assess Your Strengths, Find Your Edge, Win at Work* (Harvard Business Review Press, 2015) and several best-selling books.

PETER CAPPELLI is the George W. Taylor Professor of Management at the Wharton School and a director of its Center for Human Resources.

DENNIS CAREY is the vice chairman of Korn Ferry. He is a coauthor of *Talent Wins: The New Playbook for Putting People First* (Harvard Business Review Press, 2018) and *Go Long: Why Long-Term Thinking Is Your Best Short-Term Strategy* (Wharton Digital Press, 2018).

BEN CASNOCHA is an award-winning entrepreneur and best-selling coauthor, with Reid Hoffman, of *The Start-up of You* (Currency, 2018). He is a frequent speaker on talent management and is a coauthor of *The Alliance: Managing Talent in the Networked Age* (Harvard Business Review Press, 2014).

RAM CHARAN has been an adviser to the CEOs of some of the world's biggest corporations and their boards. He is a coauthor of *Talent Wins: The New Playbook for Putting People First* (Harvard Business Review Press, 2018).

NOSHIR CONTRACTOR is the Jane S. and William J. White Professor of Behavioral Sciences at Northwestern University, where he directs the Science of Networks in Communities research group.

PAUL R. DAUGHERTY is Accenture's chief technology and innovation officer. He is a coauthor of *Human + Machine: Reimagining Work in the Age of AI* (Harvard Business Review Press, 2018).

FRANK DOBBIN is a professor of sociology at Harvard University.

CLAUDIO FERNÁNDEZ-ARÁOZ is a senior adviser at the global executive search firm Egon Zehnder, an executive fellow at Harvard Business School, and the author of *It's Not the How or the What but the Who* (Harvard Business Review Press, 2014).

ROB GOFFEE is an emeritus professor of organizational behavior at the London Business School.

ASHLEY GOODALL is the director of leader development at Deloitte Services LP, based in New York.

REID HOFFMAN is a cofounder and the executive chairman of LinkedIn and a partner at the venture capital firm Greylock Partners. He is a coauthor of *The Alliance: Managing Talent in the Networked Age* (Harvard Business Review Press, 2014).

PAUL IRVING is chairman of the Milken Institute Center for the Future of Aging, chairman of the board of Encore.org, and a distinguished scholar in residence at the University of Southern California, Davis School of Gerontology.

GARETH JONES is a visiting professor at the IE Business School in Madrid.

ALEXANDRA KALEV is an associate professor of sociology at Tel Aviv University.

PAUL LEONARDI is the Duca Family Professor of Technology Management at the University of California, Santa Barbara, and advises companies about how to use social network data and new technologies to improve performance and employee well-being.

PATTY McCORD is the founder of Patty McCord Consulting and the former chief talent officer at Netflix.

ANNA TAVIS is a clinical associate professor of human capital management at New York University and the Perspectives editor at *People + Strategy*, a journal for HR executives.

H. JAMES WILSON is a managing director of information technology and business research at Accenture Research. He is a coauthor of *Human + Machine: Reimagining Work in the Age of AI* (Harvard Business Review Press, 2018).

CHRIS YEH is an entrepreneur, writer, and mentor. He is VP of marketing at PBworks and general partner at Wasabi Ventures. He is a coauthor of *The Alliance: Managing Talent in the Networked Age* (Harvard Business Review Press, 2014) and cofounder of Allied Talent, a consulting firm that helps organizations adopt the ideas of *The Alliance*.

Index

The most important management ideas all in one place.

We hope you enjoyed this book from *Harvard Business Review*. Now you can get even more with HBR's 10 Must Reads Boxed Set. From books on leadership and strategy to managing yourself and others, this 6-book collection delivers articles on the most essential business topics to help you succeed.

HBR's 10 Must Reads Series

The definitive collection of ideas and best practices on our most sought-after topics from the best minds in business.

- Change Management
- Collaboration
- Communication
- Emotional Intelligence
- Innovation
- Leadership
- Making Smart Decisions

- Managing Across Cultures
- Managing People
- Managing Yourself
- Strategic Marketing
- Strategy
- Teams
- The Essentials

hbr.org/mustreads

Buy for your team, clients, or event.
Visit hbr.org/bulksales for quantity discount rates.

Harvard Business Review Press